salmonpoetry

OTHER BOOKS BY BEN HOWARD

POETRY

Father of Waters: Poems 1965-1976
(Abattoir Editions: University of Nebraska at Omaha, 1979)

Northern Interior: Poems 1975-1982
(The Cummington Press, 1986)

Lenten Anniversaries: Poems 1982-1989
(The Cummington Press, 1990)

Midcentury
(Salmon Publishing, 1997)

Dark Pool
(Salmon Poetry, 2004)

Leaf, Sunlight, Asphalt
(Salmon Poetry, 2009)

PROSE

The Backward Step: Essays on Zen Practice
(Whitlock Publishing, 2014)

Entering Zen (Whitlock Publishing, 2011)

The Pressed Melodeon: Essays on Modern Irish Writing
(Story Line Press, 1996)

Firewood and Ashes
New and Selected Poems

Ben Howard

salmonpoetry

Published in 2015 by
Salmon Poetry
Cliffs of Moher, County Clare, Ireland
Website: www.salmonpoetry.com
Email: info@salmonpoetry.com

Copyright © Ben Howard, 2015

ISBN 978-1-910669-10-5

All rights reserved. No part of this publication may be reproduced or transmitted in any form or by any means, electronic or mechanical, including photography, recording, or any information storage or retrieval system, without permission in writing from the publisher. The book is sold subject to the condition that it shall not, by way of trade or otherwise, be lent, resold or otherwise circulated without the publisher's prior consent in any form of binding or cover other than that in which it is published and without a similar condition, including this condition, being imposed on the subsequent purchaser.

COVER ARTWORK: *Unveiling, (I)*, ceramic sculpture by Robin Caster Howard.
Photo by Brian Oglesbee
COVER DESIGN & TYPESETTING: Siobhán Hutson
Printed in Ireland by Sprint Print

*For Alexander, Amanda,
and Allegra*

Contents

New Poems

January First	13
Early Retirement	14
Call Me, Ishmael	15
Adagio	17
Firewood and Ashes	18
Signals	21
My First Taste of Sherry	22
Telefón Booth, Co. Cavan, 1985	23
Cloon	24
Groundhog Day	25
The Nature of Desire	26
Buson's Butterfly	27
Ugetsu	28
Magnitude	29
Darkness and Light	30
Coin of the Realm	31
Farewell to a Journal	32
Flow	33
Outpatient	34
While Waiting for the Doctor	35
Equanimity	36
Farewells	38
Maturity: A Work in Progress	39
What is This?	42
Winter and Summer	44
For Now	45
Morning Walk	46

Father of Waters (1979)

Noon	49
The Granite	50
Wild Turkey in the Rain	51
The Shale	52
Redwood	53
Lynx	55

Penelope	56
Break	57
Refuge	58
The Boar	59
Seclusion	60
In December	61
The Diver	62
Father of Waters	63
Winter Report	67

Northern Interior (1986)

Sluice	71
Fado	72
Brink	73
Figures	74
Cartographies	75
Vocation	76
Intimations	77
Cause Unknown	78
R.S.V.P	79
Criminal	80
The Woodsplitter	81
Migration	82
4 P.M.	83
Clarities	84
Letter from Iowa	85
Northern Interior	87
Two Deer	89
Span	91

Lenten Anniversaries (1990)

Monaghan Quartet	95
Small World	98
Old Men of Monaghan	99
Dublin in July	100
In Irishtown	101
Ogham	102
Ante	103
Mississippi Snappers	104

Colloquy	105
Near the Solstice	106
Lament for the Holy Places	107
Fair Exchange	108
Circlings	109
Swarming	110
Sabula	111
Fiat Lux	112
For the Calvinists	113
Losing Ground	114
Reclamation	115
MacNeice at Ithaca, 1940	116
1985	117
Because You Asked for a Bedtime Story	118
November	119
Lute Music	120
In the Regions of Belief	123
Lenten Anniversaries	124
On Reading Some of My Poems	129

MIDCENTURY (1997)

I. *The Word from Dublin, 1944*	*133*
I "I can't begin to say . . ."	133
II "The heart has many corners . . ."	134
V "Let me define . . ."	135
VI "Call it the light . . ."	136
II. *Stone on Stone*	*139*
I "I wonder . . ."	139
II "How did it happen . . ."	140
IV "And now a strangeness . . ."	141
V "There is a bitter . . ."	142
III. *The Mother Tongue*	*143*
I "With not a word . . ."	143
II "What is a mother tongue . . ."	144
IV "Mother was not . . ."	146
V "O holy longing . . ."	148

IV. Spitting Forgiven	150
I "Having a staunch affection . . . "	150
III "What is the name . . ."	152
IV "My father held his own . . ."	153
VI "Something possessed me . . ."	155
V. The Center of Attention	157
I "Across the water . . ."	157
II "Where did it begin . . ."	158
IV *"A lot of snash and blathers . . ."*	161
VI. Across the Water	163
III *"Weigh your words . . ."*	163
IV "How well the bandsmen . . ."	165
V *"Thy will be done . . ."*	166

DARK POOL (2004)

Sentence	171
Dark Pool	172
Leavings	181
Holy Water	182
Fidelities	183
Elegy	185
The Growing Poem	186
Perennials	187
Currencies	188
The Swinging Door	189
Forecast	191
Lincoln's Hands	192
A Given Name	193
Greta	195
A Winter Fire	196
Winter Night	198
Come and See	199
Prose Should Be Transparent	200
A Discipline	201
Habits	202

Necessities	203
Westward	204
Heartwood	205
The Holy Alls	206
I "How did it happen . . ."	206
II "No silence ever came . . ."	208
V "Hear it as an undulant courante . . ."	210

Leaf, Sunlight, Asphalt (2009)

The Glad Creators	215
Dublin in July	220
Beyond My Ken	223
A Wish for My Sixties	224
We Must Labor to Be Beautiful	225
Leaving Tralee	226
Original Face	227
Prune Kringle	229
The Little Drummer Boy Considers a Sabbatical	230
33 RPM	231
Leaf, Sunlight, Asphalt	232
Western New York, 2008	233
Irondequoit, Oswego, Canisteo	234
A Bow	235
One Time, One Meeting	236
"How Do You Get to Carnegie Hall?"	237
At Notre Dame	238
Expecting Nothing	239
Right Livelihood	242
Not Yet	246

Uncollected Poems

Ubi Caritas	249
The High Studio at Yaddo	252
Intrusion	253
Morning in Beara	254

New Poems

January First

While alive, be a dead person, thoroughly dead.
Then do what you will, all will be well.

      S<small>HIDO</small> B<small>UNAN</small> (1603-1676)

Dead to the world, my mother used to say,
Seeing my shoulders droop, my torso sag,
My gait diminish to a listless stumble.
Dead to the world I was, if what was meant
Was nothing more than visible fatigue,
The weathered fruit of worry and exertion.
What cared I for blooming lilac trees
Or children playing in a fragrant park?
Dead to the world I was, and little wonder.

How startling, then, to come upon an ancient
Admonition urging us to die
While still alive, as though it were a virtue
To meet the world without covert resistance
Or clamorous desire. And now what joy
To notice without prejudice or comment
This newly fallen snow on sills and railings,
As though it were the office of a dead man
To silence thought and see things as they are.

Early Retirement

Easy to take the days as they accrue,
absent a class to teach, an irony
to explicate, a question to address.
Easy to opine on happiness,
having the leisure now, if not the wisdom,
and living in a self-elected vacuum
that feels, some mornings, like a slow implosion.
And happiness? Or failing that, immersion
in gratified desire? Absent the old
intransigent demands, the days unfold,
bringing at last a little breathing room
and well-wrought thoughts to stay the rush of time.

Call Me, Ishmael

I know it might be hard for you
out there on Queequeg's coffin-buoy,
the waves lapping at its sides,
the sun beating on your skin,

to conjure out of empty air
the image of an aging man
in a distant future century
rereading after fifty years

your tale of loss and liberation.
But maybe, having watched your mates
and all your worldly obligations
sink into a self-consuming vortex,

you might be willing to reflect
on how it feels to have your props
and life-supports, your onerous
but sometimes comforting routines,

disappear quite suddenly,
revealing irrefutably
how mutable and insubstantial
they always were. In other words,

you might have something pertinent
to say about retirement,
albeit early and coerced
in your case--not a state to envy

but one from which the likes of us
who bear the name *retirees*
might learn, if only we could listen.
Your own name, which rhymes with *exile*

and means *the one whom God has heard*,
suggests you have a private line
to that omniscient, timeless Source,
who, if He should deign to speak

as well as listen, might enlighten
those of us who find ourselves
relieved of chores and useless duties
but also subject to the qualms

that come with openness, the late
discovery of vain desires.
I know you never really bought
Nantucket ideology

or thought the fierce pursuit of whales
for raw gain or fleeting glory
an emblem of maturity.
Released at last from all that strife,

your heart awakened and your mind
abrim with possibility,
you contemplate the waves that never
end, the infinite horizon.

So call us, if you will, and tell us
what you are making of your lot,
those gliding sharks your boon companions,
that rocking raft your only home.

Adagio

Call it if you must an instrument,
this meter that has served me through the decades,
its pulse an echo of my temperament,
its low-relief a match for my reserve.
But who is playing whom, I'd like to know,
feeling again the surge that would propel
the calmest, clearest mind into a maelstrom
and launch the steady heart into a vortex
where anyone could drown. In Monaghan
one April morning, I took an aimless walk,
wanting nothing more than to be rid
of aging fears and unforgiving voices.
Instead, I found the carcass of a creature,
a mess of skin and bones that might have been
a dog or newborn lamb, for all I knew.
Not what I'd expected—not at all—
nor what an April walk in search of nothing
might reasonably entail. So if I tell you
that walking steadily in prose or verse
is neither safe nor proof against disorder,
think of that ugly, desiccated body,
which, I understand, was part of nature
but nonetheless unsettled me for hours,
despite the even tempo of my steps,
the tranquil rhythm of my exhalations.

Firewood and Ashes

Firewood becomes ashes, it does not become wood again. Don't think that wood is first, ashes after . . . Life is life, death is death and are each in their own place like winter and spring. Winter does not become spring, spring does not become winter.

    Eihei Dogen

i

We cut them, one by one.
How else were we to fell
maple, beech, and ash?
One by one they dropped,
were trimmed, sawed, and hauled

to the yard beside the barn.
One by one I split
still-living limbs and trunks
and stacked them loosely, letting
fresh air circulate

between their fresh-split fibers.
How else transform a breathing
tree into a fuel
which, for good or ill,
the world calls *firewood*?

ii

We sat beside your stove
discussing this and that—
Carruth's adverse opinion
of *Walden* and Thoreau,
the merits of a life

lived, in part, alone.
That was how you liked it,
you claimed, though soon enough
your talk turned from poets
or mallards on your pond

to gossip, kind or cruel—
who said what to whom
or who was leaving whom.
And all the while your wood
was turning into ashes.

iii

Yes, we combust ourselves
from morning until night.
No action could be plainer,
no truth more evident.
But what particular loss,

need or cherished value
compelled you to combust
your mind's midnight oil
perusing students' journals,
each intimate detail

demanding your attention?
Whole weekends you went at it,
poring over stories
of drinking, drugs, abuse,
as though they were your own.

iv

Silence, you once wrote,
was what you craved the most.
Why, then, did you subject

your senses to the racket
the spring peepers made

and why did you endure
the self-imposed distractions
of Scrabble, crossword puzzles,
and always-answered calls?
What you most enjoyed,

I think, was listening,
whether what you heard
was a clear, well-chosen word
or, sometimes, a log
falling with a thud.

v

Forty years of friendship.
One by one they rise,
these memories, as if
they might resume a story
or fashion out of fire

a single breathing person.
So let those sparks arise,
and let that smoke disperse,
knowing as we do
that even firewood

does and doesn't turn
to ashes. Here and now
the flowers that you loved
are blooming near your urn
as if you still might listen.

i.m. Carol Burdick (1928-2008)

Signals

Falling through the cracks, we sometimes call it,
as though the urgent message left unanswered,
the note unread, the inquiry deleted,
had tumbled into nothingness, their substance
never to be mentioned or remembered.

And yet what signals they must send, those lost
documents and forfeited occasions,
whose stars still burn, light-years though they be
from those who might have thoughtfully responded
had they but stopped and jotted down the numbers.

My First Taste of Sherry

Remembering now my first taste of sherry
In nineteen-sixty-four, its unexpected

Sweetness and its darkness on the tongue,
I remember too the English common room

Where some of us had gathered, all of us
Younger than we knew but old enough

To recognize the transience of things.
What else, really, brought us to that room

But knowledge, conscious or unrecognized,
That we could not be twenty-one forever

And would in time become as we are now?
Reason enough to raise a glass of sherry

To youth's intuitive, unsung awareness
And also to this memory, which somehow

Hadn't occurred to me until I took
This sip of Amontillado, not so sweet

As Harvey's Bristol Cream, but capable
Of calling to mind that nearly forgotten hour.

Telefón Booth, Co. Cavan, 1985

Coin after coin, minute after minute,
the worn shillings dribble down the trough
and drop into the box. They might be divers
waiting for their turns, or paratroopers
preparing for the fall. And when they land
they make a thud, a satisfying clatter.

What have they to do with mobile phones
bleating on a crowded Dublin street
or warbling melodies in Stephen's Green?
And who are we, the ones who still recall
the cracked glass, the stiffly folding doors,
the ardors of our private conversations?

Cloon

Cluain: meadow

How well it imitates, this Irish word,
    a meadow where the phlox have gone to seed
and all that was in bloom is now in states

    of gray decline and imminent decay.
Forgive me if I savor for a while
    that one untainted melancholy vowel

    and relish as they pass those consonants
that call to mind the brittle milkweed pods,
    the sturdy grass, the stalks as yet unbroken.

Groundhog Day

Not old, not new, this February snow
that covers windshields, rails, and mounds of leaves
as though it were forgetfulness itself
and I were seeing everything anew.
Never mind that ice above the eaves,
which looks like last year's version, only larger,
and set aside that ridge vent on the roof
whose snowless line is just as I remember.
What's here are forms transformed, not old, not new,
but all the same a treasure for the eye
that takes them in, believing for a time
that all can be forgotten, all reclaimed.

The Nature of Desire

Beneath the oak the hummingbirds are sipping
their sugared water, as though they understood
the boundless nature of desire. As for
myself, I've sipped enough to know that plenty
is sometimes far too much, if what one wants
is not a life of shifting satisfactions
but something more substantial. *Don't be fooled*,
I'd tell those little birds, if my opinion
were any use at all. How beautiful
their darts and dives, their momentary squabbles,
their quick departures in the summer air.

Buson's Butterfly

Landing on the temple bell, that butterfly
Gave rise to lines that have outlasted their occasion,
Reminding you and me as we complete our breakfast
That we have no idea how a random meeting
Might still reverberate, two hundred years from now.

Ugetsu

The plotted course, the step-by-step deployment,
will ever be at odds with circumstance
and subject to the ructions of the moment.
So it was with innocent Tobei,
who left his farm to be a samurai
and Genjuro, the potter who exchanged
his wife and home for dreams of wealth and stature.

No real surprise, their brutal, sad reversals.
But what should you and I, so far removed
from feudal wars, infer from their misfortunes?
Here in mid-September, rinsed by rain,
the pink impatiens bloom among the sedum
and nesting geese, whatever our intentions,
look out above the grass, unmoved, unfrightened.

Magnitude

This evening as I look out on those stars
Of sundry magnitudes above the tree line,
I'm thinking of the morning, decades past,

When a book arrived unbidden in my mailbox.
A new anthology of poetry,
It featured, in the back, a black-and-white

Two-page image of a nighttime sky.
A Galaxy of Poets, it was called,
Each poet's name in white Helvetica,

Its font determined by the poet's stature.
Truth to tell, vanity prevailed,
And after a time I found my forlorn name

In the smallest possible font, and, worse than that,
Barreling toward the crack between the pages.
I'm sorry to report that I was miffed

Though now, thirty years on, I have to wonder
Why I wasn't pleased, or better, grateful
To be present in that company at all.

What is maturity if not this knowledge,
However incomplete, that rest will come
Only when that lust for magnitude

Is seen for what it is? I read them now,
Those names that might be avenues or lanes,
Crescents or thoroughfares, and note how many

Major or minor stars have since departed,
Leaving behind their names, which even now
Retain a glow of consequence and ardor.

Where have they gone? I ask, imagining
A universe where all are of a piece
And all bright stars of equal magnitude.

Darkness and Light

The darkness around us is deep.
    William Stafford

Still and all, Stafford kept on going,
morning after morning at his table.

I see him now, sitting in my armchair,
eyes half-closed, resting his fertile mind.

You never know, he told me once in passing,
where, when you shoot it, a bullet will end up.

May he rest, whose mind so seldom rested,
probing as it did the world's unending darkness.

Coin of the Realm

Keep it to yourself, we used to say

when privacy was like a secret letter
tucked between the folds of disused linens
and never spoken of, much less detected.

No one needs to know, we said and meant,

when privacy was held in such esteem
it might have been a family's only heirloom
worth passing on, its only gold or silver.

Don't tell a soul, our elders darkly warned,

as if by saying that they might protect
the one remaining coin in their possession
or keep intact a bright unsullied name.

Farewell to a Journal

What concerns me now
is what you don't contain.
Not the momentary,
furtive recognition.
Not the dream abandoned
at seven in the morning,
its images too brutal
to keep or contemplate.
Not the sidelong glance
at losses too profound
to register or grieve,
lest their reality
become a lightless pit,
their truth a stopping point.
Instead, you hold intact
my daily cogitations,
worries, plans, directives,
as though a single life
could be explained at last
by accurate description,
precise analysis,
or news of changing weather.

Flow

Intelligence, it seems, is neither warder
nor wise protector when it comes to houses.
Listen, if you can, to water seeping
into your old foundation. Where it goes
your earnings go, as does your peace of mind.
Listen to water dripping from your eaves
and hope that every downspout, every gutter
is as it should be, water knowing how
to find its way, even through block and mortar.
And if it is your habit to solicit
divine assistance, pray for competence
in all the crafts pertaining to construction,
lest the element your body's made of,
the one that can undo you by its absence,
should prove to be your enemy, intent
on turning all your hours and your labor
to sand and mud, and all your good intentions
into a lesson that you duly learned
but somehow in maturity forgot,
its best reminder seeping from a crack
that might be patched, though what persists behind it
will ever be at odds with your containment.

Outpatient

Infirmity, that onyx-hearted beast,
arrives with age, the two of them determined

to meddle with the flesh and leave the rest
dispirited, unstable, undermined.

No matter, I would so much like to say.
The beast is not a predator, exactly,

despite its claws, its gross rapacity.
I'd like to call its insults merely nature

acting as it must. I'd like to throw
worry to the winds and let its seeds

supply the multitudes that come and go.
To note but not to dwell on what occurs:

let that be my intention for today,
my infant thought, hidden amid the reeds.

While Waiting for the Doctor

Better, I thought, to lift my downcast eyes,
surveying what I'd hitherto ignored.
The rubber bulb hanging from its bracket.
The tongue depressors, cotton swabs; the outlets
covered with safety plugs, as though a toddler
might at any time insert an object.

At any time: that phrase could be a mantra
reminding us that anything can happen.
Let's say that you were walking down the sidewalk,
not seeing how irregular it was.
You didn't fall. Not then and not thereafter,
though anything can happen anytime.

Equanimity

Today I'm standing firm
Or rather trying to stand

Firmly on this contraption
Known as a BOSU Ball.

A blue hemisphere
Rising from the floor,

It might be half a planet
Or, more plausibly,

The deep blue sea.
Do thirty squats, he ordered,

My fit PT instructor,
Who looks as if he might

On a good day do three hundred.
Can he begin to imagine

How it might feel to be
Thirty-five years his senior?

Yes, I think he can,
Which is why he's having me

Perform these thirty squats,
Reluctantly but ably.

Why blue? I have to wonder.
Is it to promulgate

The amiable delusion
That this is California

And I am all of twenty
Riding the blue Pacific,

Blissfully unaware
Of how unsure this life is

And how we so easily fall?
I mustn't think of that.

I'm up to twenty-five
And still intact, a fact

That might amuse the gods
Of youth and youthful beauty.

Let them make their jokes
Or offer up, in faintly

Condescending tones,
Their wish for my success.

Grateful to be possessed
Of all my limbs and marbles,

I'm happy to be squatting
On this blue unstable ball,

As on this hurtling planet,
Which also holds us up,

We young and old alike,
For as long as we are able.

Farewells

Even as the days are growing longer
they're passing by with such rapidity
they might be water hurtling down a mountain.
Tell me if you will why names and dates,

which seem so static in the histories,
are rushing past this stationary point
as though they had a mission that concerned me
but all the same were bidding me farewell.

Maturity: A Work in Progress

1

Where are the poems I had thought to write
in this the shaded grove of my retirement?
Call it what you will, that longed-for respite
has brought humility if not atonement
for blunders, oversights, and covert lies
which seemed but ways of coping at the time.
But where, if anywhere, are my entreaties
to whatsoever power might redeem
my early follies? Where my elegies
for youth or middle age or reckless passion?
Today my thoughts and unleashed energies
are weighing images, as is their fashion,
in search of who knows what enabling theme.
If lines should be the fruit of that adventure,
then let those lines depict without erasure
such scenes as language can or cannot redeem.

2

What are the wages of a faulty marriage?
That afternoon, it might have been an arrow,
her caustic taunt. It was more than I could manage.
To keep the faith, to walk the Straight and Narrow,
is fine enough, but let's not kid ourselves:
to err is human, even when the stakes
are higher than the highest warehouse shelf
and no less treacherous. We make mistakes
and break each other's spirits while we're at it.
So who was in the right or in the wrong?
Who was being good and who erratic?
What matters now, those dust-ups long since gone,
is not the portioning of blame or praise
but whether it be possible at last
to set aside those lenses, which have cast
for forty years their colors on our days.

3

In the grey light of due consideration
the bile-inflected putdown seems remote
and bland passivity a mild condition.
It wasn't so. Those arguments, played out
against a backlit history of loss,
destroyed whatever *caritas* remained
after the first coarse shout. Contemptuous
and condescending, arrogant and drained
of any true incentive to continue,
we kept it up, that inconclusive struggle,
not seeing what its ugliness might do
to one we truly loved. We learned to haggle
but not to put an end to all such noise.
How gratifying, now, to write such words
as might, in time, atone for cruel deeds
and open passageways to future joys.

4

How can we tell a symptom from a cause,
especially in matters of the heart?
Late in the afternoon, I think it was,
when she stood still, preparing to depart.
Beside her stood my son, his hand in hers.
Was it a symptom, that internal pain,
which would recur, the months becoming years,
as if to say again and yet again
that bonds of flesh and blood could not suffice
to staunch whatever hemorrhage had commenced,
unchecked, untreated? Call it the slow release
of each lost Parents' Day, each missed performance,
the casual and everyday communion
of son and father. May these verses be,
for all their poverty and imperfection,
those hours' late, unsteady elegy.

5

Is it not a con, that bogus notion
that all of us are victims of each other?
Today the victim's Jane, tomorrow John.
And all the while we're making heavy weather
of each new slight, each real or misconstrued,
exploitable affront within our fiefdoms.
So let me skim away that yellowed curd
and sip the milk of truth, if not of wisdom.
And let me now recall the well-known yarn
of the boatman in his still unblemished boat
who struck another of a foggy morning.
Irate, irrational, he threw a fit,
only to find the other boat was empty
and therefore void of consciousness or story.
I dwelt in ignorance, as people do,
and so did she. What more is there to say?

6

Let it begin, this heartfelt act of courage,
this fortunate departure. Here on the eve
of a son's auspicious entry into marriage,
let ancient grievances unclench themselves
and petty spites be buried with their handles.
What unresolved dispute or unhealed cut
in any one of us can hold a candle
to this impersonal transforming rite
that gives the lie to self-inflicted rancor?
In truth, those bitter scenes to which my mind
so readily returns are neither here
nor anywhere, their drama long since ended.
Before us lies this luminous commencement,
which summons us to listen and allow
remembered injuries to be but straw
in these the fires of the present moment.

What is This?

For Alexander and Amanda
  June 5, 2011

When we took a leisurely walk
Around your neighborhood
One sunny afternoon

We paused at a stranger's yard.
What caught your joint attention
Was, itself, a stranger:

A green, globular fruit
Suspended from a vine.
You stopped to study it,

Questioning again
And again what it might be,
As though the mystery

Of all things yet unknown,
Unnamed, unclassified,
Had gathered in that yard.

As, indeed, it had.
And as the two of you
Extended into pure

Nothingness your lines
Of thought, not yet converging
But not diverging either,

You became not two, not one.
And what I would wish for you
Is not the enraptured gaze

Into each other's eyes
But that congruent look
At what the passing world

Is beckoning you to see.
What is *this*? I would bid you
Ask of what you meet,

Whether it be a fruit
Or fragrant foreign plant
Or inexplicable child.

Winter and Summer

When will it end, this yearning to be elsewhere?
Come mid-June, I will be sixty-nine.
In the same month, as if to blunt that fact,
a long-awaited grandchild will be born.
No greater joy—and, in truth, no better
reason to be exactly where I am.
Why, then, this infant longing to repeat
the past or throw a lifeline to the future?
To live in another climate-zone or time?
Will she be blonde, or will her hair be brown?
Whom will she resemble? *Wait and see*,
I tell myself, as if that might allay
this urge to hold a child not yet born
and trade midwinter for a summer's day.

For Now

For now it is enough to watch the blue jays
    and to catch a whiff of sandalwood arising
in the morning air. Enough to note the shallow
    puddles left on the deck from last night's rain
and to feel against my wrist the touch of hemp,
    which is neither coarse nor soft, stiff nor supple,
but something in between. *Be positive,*
    said Hemingway, not meaning to uplift
our laden hearts or maketh us lie down
    in pastures conjured from our hearts' desires,
but rather to enjoin us to take heed
    of what is here, eschewing what is not.
How right he was, I think, hearing the traffic's
    pulsing din, the dove's disconsolate vowel.

Morning Walk

What will make me happier, I wonder:
telling tales in my advancing years,
tales of my mistakes and second guesses,

or setting those depleted sticks on fire
and storing in the darkness of my coffers
their soft, unsifted, unexamined ashes?

What will I bequeath to my descendents,
who have no need or place for storied urns
or uses for the dust contained therein?

Just this, I think: the not-yet-labeled scents
encountered on a walk. The feel of stones
beneath my feet. The sudden windborne rain.

Father of Waters

(1979)

Noon

Early morning shadows deepen ruts
    and darken scars. They fill the veins
  of leaves still wet with dew
    and swell a coffee cup into
a club, menacing saucer and spoon,
    and follow a duck across wet grass,
stretching its bill and tail till they become

two grizzled snouts. In these
    uncomplicated shapes, which catch
only the bulk and breadth of what
    they follow, seldom its feather and quill,
one sees the mind's own flat
    persistent shadow
trailing behind the things which it desires,

distending head and limb. Yet one looks out
    in an early morning hour such as this one,
watching a sparkling grackle land
    upon a roof, and one imagines noon,
when every object clarifies itself
  in sunlight, void of mind and shadow,
and is itself alone, a thick
    beak, or iridescent wing.

The Granite

The granite has no bones and no remains

Its hollows are the habitudes of shadows
No eyes reside there

No mouth
No flat black crack

The granite lingers where the soil has been

It holds its own among the clouds
The eagles
The white plateaus

The granite has no poor relations
No family ties
No maiden aunts and no

Religion

It holds its own among the fountains

Wild Turkey in the Rain

His wattle drips like tallow down
his neck. His head, a wet
shaft of ash, protrudes

above the reeds. His eye
looks back across the lake, as though
his enemy were water. Breast

erect, his feathers lie
like strata, each a ledge
over which a stream

is plunging. Now he swells
his lungs, thrusts out
his sides in a soft

explosion. Splinters and bits
of bark fly out and flames
shoot up behind him, spreading across

the leaves, the moist
branches and piles
of stones. The shallow pools
ripple; his feathers close.

The Shale

The shale disintegrates when water
Rushing across it like the robes
Of judges carries it along.

Because the shale
Is soft its elements keep company
With cans and rotting fishing-lines and vines
The catch the little splinters in their course
Like bits of meat between
Two tines.

The shale accepts the verdict,
Letting itself be riven by the stream
On which its plenitude
Depends. Its elements

Keep company with rivulets
That wander and meander like the ruts
On judges' brows.

Redwood

For all its hardiness it's soft
    as pine, as malleable
  as balsa. Red
      as cowhide it seems brighter, less
        enslaved to brown. Its grain has neither
      broken lines like oak nor waves
        like walnut. One imagines
    curtains, slightly parted at the knot,
fold on fold. And one detects
    shadows between the folds and blades

the shape of knives.
    The knives
  are neither lethal nor
    erratic. Side by side,
      as on a cutting board, they seem
    harmless as garter snakes, their heads
  converging at the knot. They seem
as slim as eels, asleep

in a redwood sea.
    If one should press
  one's hand against these knives,
    should press quite firmly down,
  the wood and not one's hand
would suffer. Soft
  and fragile, every seam
would soon give way. The yearly
layers would separate like seeds,
  or families after feuds, and go

their separate ways.
    If one should ask
  what power, what
    miraculous cohesion held these layers,
      year on year, together, kept

      this entity intact,
         one might be struck to realize
    that it was just that force whose slight
and local evidence one
       had just destroyed. Sabers and shields would swim
     before one's eyes.

Lynx

His fur resembles waves
of leaves, under which a wind

is heaving. White
and dry, his lighter hair

seems nearer winter,
scattered across his coat

like frosted straw. Beneath
his mouth, like ice beneath

a crevice, lies
his beard. It is as cold

as the white rings around
his eyes, which now begin

to close, as might
the rings of frost around

a stem: the mouth
of winter.

Penelope

I tell you again that she believed in him.
What is there but belief? She knew so little.
Hordes of stories invaded her, not one

To be believed. That he was captured, maimed,
Or stabbed with a hundred knives was not beyond
Belief. But she could credit only what

She saw, and she saw nothing, year after year.
So she believed in nothing—nothing except
Ulysses, and his eventual return.

And so she became two women: one who believed
And one who had abandoned all belief.
Did the years deceive her? And when he returned, at last,

Did all her incredulity take flight?
I wish that it were so. But when he spoke
Of love and of the women he had known

But never loved, of vows and self-denial—
And when he pledged his final years to her
Alone, only a part of her believed.

Break

Over an oil drum the workmen warm
Their hands. The riveter and welder come
From across the yard, picking up sticks and bits
Of coal to feed the fire. The hookup men
Pull off their greasy leather gloves and join
The circle, standing quietly among
The men who drive the forklifts, pack the trucks
And tear the crates apart. Above them, cranes
Are winding down. The fire spits and pops
And throws up yellow flames beyond the rim.

Is that the cry of quail? Some silver strands
Of smoke are rising, past the faces caked
With dirt, the forearms wet with oil. No
Quail in here. No hawk or falcon either.
Only the clang of steel, the reamer's cleats
Crunching the rock and sand. Only freight cars
Coupling and uncoupling endlessly
In the other yard. The grizzled foreman rocks
Back and forth, and back, and bows his head,
Watching fire as other men watch water.

Refuge
for Loren Eiseley

Winter has stilled the ice but cannot hold
   the mind to the present moment. One remembers
the purple mallow close to the soil,
   the elderberry clumps like small umbrellas
and the nest of frost, its flakes as thin
   as flies' wings. Winter has stopped the water-pipe
and snow the thickness of a woolen scarf
   wraps the ash and maple. Still, the mind
turns inward, recalling the pigeons' flight
   from the silo, the killdeer's flash
of white. A sudden glint
   from a tin truss returns
the eye to outward voyages. Yet that light
   soon fails, and shingles blur
as one takes refuge in an incident
   long past, a moment in an alley
or a day in a foreign village.
   It is all that one can do to watch the stems
bending before the window.

The Boar

For four long years I lived with him
As though he were my mother or my father
Or my family all in one. The men had knocked
His upper teeth out, leaving his tusks to curl
In the smooth crescent of a quarter moon
Over his snout and down until they pierced
His leathery skin. Their white stalks swelled
And lengthened, bending toward the windows of
His eyes. And all the while, sequestered there

Among those boys, uprooted from my home,
I too was growing. I watched my limbs increase
And heard my vowels deepen. I was alone,
Surrounded though I was by elbows, knees,
And shoulders bony as mine. And when my voice
Cracked, and I was buffeted by laughter,
I turned my face away. At night, I looked
To the wall, and saw my mother's face rise up
And heard her calling. Meanwhile, that animal

Panted and rooted in his filthy pen
And glowered, trusting in no one, least of all
In me. I fed him grain and table scraps
And watched the bristles rising on his back
Like my own first hair; and pelted him
With stones when he wouldn't move. I saw the lust
That drove him around the pen and back again
And yet was no more urgent than my own.
I heard his anger, vented in snorts and groans.

And then it ended. Three of us took him out
And slit his throat. And everyone was there
To watch, as though the cutting of his throat
Were the cutting of a cord which bonded me
To him and them, whose flesh had come to seem
My flesh, and would not let go. And so I left them,
Taking unto myself the strength that once
Was his and mine; and leaving, once and for all,
That mass of bloodied mud and twisted bone.

Seclusion

This far away the days run off like water

This distance is a stone
Which one would lift if one were able

Which one would push aside
Discovering ants and regiments of worms
Crawling through strands and filaments to find
Seclusion

This far away
The days run off like water from the grain
And haywagons come and go
Like ships down the wet stone road

In December
for Dan Davidson

The river's heart is jubilant and wild.
It beats beneath the ice-encrusted vines
And pumps its dark beneficence to bald,
Protruding branches
And sucks its praises from the slime.

At sunset children skate upon an altar.
Red winter clouds hang down.
The fishermen in vestments, gold and blue,
Let down their lines.

In the night the savage divers come with knives
And swim in loops around the bulging core.

The Diver

Listen, listen, and draw near:
Love is inexhaustible and full of fear.

       DELMORE SCHWARTZ

He can't remain forever underwater,
Feeling his lungs contract and his shoulders tire
From pulling against a force which like a door
That will not open might induce despair

In one less willing to be compromised
By a power which he's never understood
Or dragged downstream, powerless and deprived
Of any willful course he might have had,

All for the sake of catching once or twice
A glimpse of elements unknown to him,
Which float in the dark and silence like the face
Of one in whose confusion he became

A self outside himself, and again a man,
Spent and cleansed in a chaos not his own.

Father of Waters

i

To what, my friend, have you
Returned?

By day, your father's nets stretched
Upon a wooden reel,
White wisps rising from the smokehouse,
Wet buckets filled with carp—

By night, the barges hauling steel and coal
And the towboats wailing,
Hurling their white lights upon
Four walls—

For you there is no
Religion now, no Holy Ghost,
No black-frocked preacher promising
Salvation.

Your father's mottled hand chops
The heads from carp and catfish.
Your mother's wrist
Quivers upon the table.

ii

In a flat-bottomed fishing-boat that smells of oil

You go out at six o'clock to run
The lines. Your father
Holds in his right hand a dripping gar
Whose row of teeth turns pink.

In the rising sun.
And you remember

Your laughing father standing over the river
And your own soft face afloat
Amid the sticks and cans.

It is a man's
Unshaven face that greets you
Now, from the lapping water,

You, who heard the drone
Of the late-night plane to Chicago
And one day followed—

          The old man calls
For help. You feel
The lurch when the bulging net is lifted over

And watch the carp
Jump, their bodies flashing,

As though the two of you had taken ore
From water.

   iii

"I am no river lover,"
She said, and swore
She'd never live there.

But that's exactly what she's done
For forty years, and you,
Her son, have listened

To stories of trappers drowned
Beneath the barges, stories
Of fishermen struck
By lightning.

        Shapes

Would rise and swell upon your wall,
The shapes of men,
Their knees drawn up against
Their chests, men stretched out
On sand—

And her voice in the dark would tremble,

*May the Good Lord bless
And keep thee.*

    iv

Your young son tugs
On the rope and brings the seine

Around. Fourteen hundred pounds
Of buffalo harvested
By noon. And in the tank
The catfish thrashing—

        To this have you
Returned, bringing
A boy of ten,
Who leaps from a wrecked barge, goes down,

And comes up splashing, kicking against
Dark water. Far
Downriver, sturgeon, paddlefish, catfish pass
Heedlessly into the dam—

In the shadow of the barge
He walks, your mother's image in his eyes,
Your son who will not be drowned,

Whose voice will never tremble,

Walks waist-high in water,

Spreading his arms as thought he held up clouds,
As though the clouds pressed down

Upon his shoulders.

v

And neither Son
Nor Holy Ghost resides

In the black water slapping the little skiff
As a barge comes down the river.

Yet you return, as to a Scripture,

And watch the water part before the prow
Of the barge, where numbers painted
In white become the rungs
Of a ladder reaching down—

Beneath cold stars
The towboat's beacon turns,
Scanning the sloughs and sandbars with its slow

White light.

O river river—

Agates and catfish.
On and on.

i.m. Marion Howard 1905-1971

Winter Report

The world is several billion years of age
   and I am thirty. Last year's grass
Comes up like whiskers through the snow
   and the shovel leans against the barn.
And I am weary, weary of metaphor,
   of making from the residue of thought
a gathered whole. And what is gathered?
   Surely not the fantasies that spring
from a pile of bricks imagined as a building,
   nor the memories that cling
to padlocks, stumps, old cable. All
   is wrapped, tied, presented whole
to those who believe in wholes, or wish to.
   And the voices speaking quietly
backstage, the doubts and questions rising in
   the mind, remain unheard
by any reader. This fine deception
   can't go on. The bright sunlight falls
on the ice at the peak of a roof
   but doesn't melt it. The roof itself
is bent. And the thing which only a moment ago
   I'd thought to say, is already fled and gone.

Northern Interior

(1986)

Sluice

The curled stone at the edge
   Of the garden catches failing light
As a pitcher water. What shall a word
   Catch, its fragility
No match for clay or stone?
   To the failing light repeat
The name of water. As though it flowed
   Through a cracked dike, the water
Opens a sluice and soon escapes
   The word that held it. Failing light
Falls on the colloquy of rain and stone,
   As on that sluice, which is neither wind nor water.

Fado

for Joanne Mensinger

Water is not intelligent
But what this rain is saying to the screen
And the wicker furniture
Is, in its own way, wise.
It has kept its sermon up for hours.
To the drooping rhododendrons
It has urged a sturdier detachment
And a keener sense of danger.
To the bicycles, the garden tools,
And the car's neglected windows
It has recommended foresight.
And to us, two children watching
Droplets splattering the pavement,
It has counseled stoical
Endurance. Whether by chance
Or by design, our lives will not
Grow straight. Transplanted, pruned,
And torn, we will not remember
Every calamity we suffer
Or recall each tangible
Delight. Or so we are told by water
Falling from troughs and fenders,
As though it had heard our stories in its own
Tattoo on boards and railings
Or read our errors in its thin,
Divergent lines.

Brink

After the cold
light of March
the first leaves
of the crabapple
open, the cherry's
branches thicken.
Another winter
dwindles as if
it had never begun.

The scars stay:
broken shale,
the split plank.
All day one waits
for certainties,
as though the wear
of eave and trough,

cheek and hand,
might be forestalled:
as though this sense
of falling forward,
helpless and cold
were but a sly
illusion. Rich

in loss, replete
with winter's bitterness,
the earth receives
our misplaced hope
and vain desire.
Look: new growth
on the yew, new color
nurtured in damp remains.

Figures

It ended. After the coldest months
the ice cracked; the channel opened.
There was no more crossing except by boat.

Up till then we made our marks—
circles, crescents, scars—wherever
we could, and usually at random.

Never mind that some of us were good
or purposeful. The river won,
as it always had; and what we kept

was what we carried in ourselves
to another winter: figure-eights
and fancy stops—or just mistakes

which even the river couldn't erase
or break into splinters, or call its own.

Cartographies

Unsummoned, uncontainable,
The new day enters through a slot
In broken blinds. The morning forecast

Wakens us to a world of crisp
Or not-so-crisp divisions, edges,
Places and dates, as if to say

That the night's vivid fluidity
Was only another wilderness,
An island of memory, remorse,

And florid imaginings, which someone
Wiser than ourselves would leave
Behind. We listen attentively

To such advice. But in the space
Mapped by the weatherman, the mountains
Carved by sinuous demarcations,

We sense another wilderness
Crossing forbidden lines. We look
Faithfully at the boundaries

Of states, the signatures of rivers,
And the outlines of the continent
We call our own. Yet in the yard

Outside our window, maple leaves
Will not hold still, and wayward light
Riddles the bark of moving branches.

Vocation

The hay is dry. And in their innocence
   Two pheasants sun themselves
In the quiet amplitude of late July.
   One wonders where such calm
Originates, and what toothed beasts
   Lie under. Here is the mind's
Fork in the road: for one might choose
   To skate upon appearances'
Recumbent skin—or choose to turn
   Inward, churning up lethal snakes,
Spiders, worms, and who knows what
   Pernicious cluster. To peel back bark,
Lift rocks, and rake
   The skein of complacency from things:
That is the mind's peculiar
   Vocation. And yet what still
And cool elation
   The stirrings of consciousness perturb and conquer.

Intimations

i

    At times I ask a question.
an unassuming question,
that opens like a canyon,
stark, uncharted,
into which one must descend, if only
to move ahead, despite the steep
and narrow path,
whose colors make suggestions
too subtle to understand,
though one might chip a sample
to study or show a friend
should one come home.

ii

    And at times I hear a note
that is like a cello's but not so lasting,
a note too low for singing,
as though the cellist's bow had struck a rock,
a lump of granite,
and sent a tremor through the soil,
till I know I am not secure
whether I stand my ground
or run for cover that is never there
but seems to be, as clouds sometimes
resemble tents and silos.

Cause Unknown

Smoke circulates
round orange embers, half-obscuring
their boulderlike remains. Ridges and palisades,

rows of blackened vertebrae
in the log's back, fossils in glowing coals:
such sightings are improbable

but true. And true the memory
they conjure: sunlight caught in the teeth of the gar,
sparks from the welder's torch, the charred

residual spine
of a neighbor's hand-hewn beam. No use to take
precautions. No use against such force, or against

that other fire: the row of flames
that look like teeth, the blue acetylene ring
within. Whole nations burn

because of it: friendships, families, clans
lost like infants sacrificed
to Isis. Think of the living

body of Shadrach
pushed into the furnace like a letter
whose message is obscure. And later,

the inspector sifting ashes, thinking *arson*
but citing *cause unknown*
to the slowly dispersing crowd.

R.S.V.P.

To step into nature is to wrap
a cold coat—the one left out
on the porch—around oneself

and go out in the wind for cordwood.
We have no choice. This planet
has never loved us. To leap beyond

oneself: that is the invitation
the bark keeps making. And here we are,
grinding our wedges, keeping our axes sharp.

Criminal

Sometimes a man falls away
from the others like a stone. To honor him,
we pretend it's erosion or an accident

of nature. Where he was, the sky
turns a darker hue. We go on plowing snow
from our driveways, keeping

our eyes on the blade.
Sometimes we strike a rock, reminding us
of him. There is no other way we can go.

The Woodsplitter
for William Underhill

He will never find in wood the worm that gnaws
the brain, nor in steel the implement of bile
though the wood be split, and further split, and though
the steel he swings be charged by such a force

as springs from knowledge that would break a will
less stern than his, knowledge that like a bow
bent fully back, recoils beneath the stress,
only to be restrained by the will's replies.

Yet it will give release to see bright steel
plunge into strands of ash as into marrow
and to see between those strands no human face
but a severed bond, and to deal inhuman blows

to wood whose every filament is wild
and splits most cleanly when it is most cold.

Migration

This white intuitive light
falls on an altered landscape.
The ditch that carried water

off the field is filled
with dirt and stone. The land
is not what it was, nor is

our orchard permanent.
This light is finding rifts
in the soil, and each new walk

turns up another mound
or carcass. One day we'll leave
this field, and take this light

to a place with high,
unalterable hills,
if we can find it. Walking

north, we'll feel the knolls
unseating themselves, the creeks
spreading their rocks behind us.

4 P.M.

Yes: you will walk that alley again,
passing the same backyards, the same
fences and gardens, the same unpainted
posts. But something fortuitous

and new will get in the way: a gate
you have never seen; an elder tree
grown tall; a stand of hollyhocks . . .
Whatever it is, it will throw its long

shadows across the lawn. And when
the once-familiar gables darken,
as if from aging or too much rain,
and wary strangers come to their doors,

you will cry out silently, unsure
of where you have lived or who you are.

Clarities

You find your way. One of the streets
   Has lost its name, and still another
Turns, as if to violate
   Your recollection. You did not expect
To see your neighbors or to rest
   Assured. You came here hoping
To map those districts in yourself
   Whose lines lie broken or indistinct,
Even as speech is slurred. And yet,
   Lost among gates and fences,
You see how little such a search
   Can clarify, how few
The demarcations. Look: at the corner of
   Your eye, the white uncluttered line
Of an unfamiliar gable. There,
   If anywhere, resides that clarity
You came for. Beside that sober line
   The door you closed and opened as a child
Is now a blur. And yet you couldn't find
   That strange distinctness anywhere but here.

Letter from Iowa

for James Benfield

    Not many people come
to this bluff above the river.
In winter the limestone ledge
turns white and precarious.
Over the limestone wall
the northern wind comes climbing—
mischievous, capricious,
and frightening to children.

    Today the wind has fled
to wherever northern winds
flee in the heat of August,
and the ledge beneath our feet
is like a serving platter
or the brass collection-plate
in the story you told me once—
the plate left by an usher
on a steaming radiator
while the minister droned on.

    In the yellow dust, our footprints
mingle and cross, becoming
crazed and indistinct.
In the pool above the dam
the river's undulant weight
is making the *Saratoga*,
with its noisy diesel engines,
its fifteen loaded barges,
seem still and small.

    It would seem the Mississippi
is pulling its usual trick
of making the rest of us
feel less than consequential.

    But today, to cheer myself,
I think how that story ended:
the absent-minded usher,
who was also a bassist, carried
the hot plate up to the altar.
His calloused fingers felt
no pain. And at the altar
the representative
of God's mysterious will
received the offering,
but not for long. His hands
flew upward, flinging pledges
into the waiting air.
On the varnished pews, the quarters,
pennies, and nickels skipped
like stones on devouring water.

Northern Interior
for Wyatt Prunty in Virginia

   Wyatt, here in this Northern state
the air is turning colder. Cars go by
with their windows half-rolled-up; unwelcome chills
circle my collar. Down in the South, I'm told,
        the planet is less formidable,

   even in October. Here,
the maples seem incapable of warmth
or any sort of rapture. Now their bark—
furrowed, speckled with lichen—binds them tight
        and seems an emblem for that habit

   of holding back—that reticence
which, for all our difference, we share.
Think of the voice that cautions and commands us
in sleep, as in those frightful confrontations
        where, if there were no voice, we might

   savage our cherished principles
or burn our houses down. Today that voice
grows all too loud. It calls in a vacant room,
echoes across the hall. I'd like to tell you
        where it first was heard, and where

   it learned its curious, insular
restraint. All I will say is that its cry
grows more insistent now, in mid-October,
and that the honkings of the wild geese
        are not more doleful or familiar.

   Perhaps the migratory birds
are telling me a truth I might have learned
from the blue flames warming the blackened pan,
the yellow foliage burning away the mist,
        the steam above the woodshed. Trust

  is costly, yet in its absence one
lives in a frigid wilderness, a state
from which one ventures warily, prepared
for quick retreat. I know where I have lived
   and where I must. And yet the thought

  of winter wakens an old desire
to find a more hospitable interior,
a latitude less austere. I'd like to trust
to instinct, letting it lead me southward. There,
  if you were willing, we might trust

  to friendship, knowing how readily
it fails. As one whose ancestors were Vikings,
I should not be averse to frozen rivers
of the tight face fighting tears. And yet some days
  I am. I trust you will understand.

Two Deer
for L.E.

      Again, Loren, the middle of August
finds me aghast with how little I've done. The swallows
fledged in their muddy nest above the yard-lamp
over a month ago and flew away.
      At least they accomplished something. I

    can claim no similar achievement.
Even the hay fared better than I: it grew—
drenched in three weeks' rain—and finally
was cut. I know, like me, you've felt that vague
      illicit desire to be less

    than human: perhaps to be a fox
or one of the steers in our pasture, nosing a fencepost,
chewing a handful of grass, achieving nothing.
Accomplishment, I fear, is a human invention,
      designed to keep the likes of you

    and me in a state of anxiety
or joy. Where did we find our need to build
edifices of words to prove our worth,
as if such structures were a "stay against
      confusion," yes, but also against

    oblivion, waste, and ruin? You
have known all three, and more. I think of you
thumping the floor to signal to your mother—
your mother, deaf and dumb—or running away
      from the woman she'd become: a mad,

    wild Fury chasing her son
across a cornfield. You say you cannot recall
whether you laughed at her. But did you see
yourself as her in thirty years, a grown
      man, fronting the taunting faces?

    Perhaps achievement is a house,
a sturdy house, immune to ridicule.
It seems that I've been building such a house
for years, as though I had no other aim
        than to avoid becoming one

   whom insolent sons might jeer and shake
a stick at. Nobler purposes we have,
I'm sure. But August is disintegrating,
and tonight I feel inclined to let it go.
        It was only yesterday I lay

   in the hammock, watching the light go out
of the hawthorns on the hill. I heard, behind me,
a little noise, and then I saw the deer—
young; quick ears; dark eyes—not twenty feet
        away. I wish you had seen them, Loren;

   but if words are good for anything,
they are right for re-articulating what
the world has put together, bone by bone.
I write to tell you that I saw two deer.
        For a moment, they and I were still.

Span

She moves from pane to pane
To watch the wary does
Stepping out of the ditch
And onto the lighted roadbed
Where, for a while, they walk
In the dangerous lanes, their tails
Reddened by morning light
Till they seem to look her back
And to lead her watery eyes
Like fawns to the other side.

Lenten Anniversaries

(1990)

Monaghan Quartet

i.m. Patrick Kavanagh (1904-1967)

1 Openings

On sodden days the wind returns in gusts,
blasting the rhododendrons. Here in the north,
late April's wild recovery advances
in the wet fields, bearing along old doubts
and fresh misgivings. Out of these morning mists
will come a clarity, a second birth,
a shining. Or so I announce—and take my chances
against a force that throws its coiled nets
over the gorse, the piled stones, the hedgerows.
This mist will lift. Those tangled roots and fibers
beneath the rocks, those skeins of memory,
will be unearthed beneath a northern light
that renovates old posts and casts new shadows
into the pools and furrows. Out of our fears
will come a strength, and out of a lengthening story
will rise a hierarchy of worth, a plot,
and understanding. Or so we assure ourselves,
seeing the truth and error of our ways
in newly parted clouds, in flights of crows
performing slow ascents and savage dives.

2 Monaghan

This torn county spares itself the frowns
of tourists, the foreigners' aspersions. Small,
unwatched, the primrose brightens in the ditch;
the holly hones its edges. Bound for Fermanagh,
visitors might inspect these greystone towns
and whin-crowned drumlins once, or not at all—
the slopes too gentle, the fields too close to catch
the eye. Here are the black hills Kavanagh
renounced, the wayside nettles that snagged his spirit.

Stranger to a landscape he found common,
I ride uneasily on borrowed roads
and meet, at pillbox checkpoints on the border,
a specter Kavanagh never saw. The light
that falls impartially on Ireland's pain
and felicity, falls here on barricades,
a slot of glass, a corrugated bunker,
a civil and detested soldiery.
Near to a line where old disunions fester
and tribes convene, this severed wing of Ulster
shadows its own, who call it bandit country.

3 Annaghmakerrig

Victorian floorboards creak beneath the weight
of comings and goings, the fretfulness of writers
walking the mirrored halls. To put the Big House
up for adoption! And to watch these rooms
giving themselves to strangers! If we should ferret
out of these storied walls unopened letters,
secrets and untold tales, each routed voice—
ranting or whispering, intoning rhymes
or muttering curses through a mask of virtue—
would lure us out of the halls' protective light
and into our private rooms, where lambent motives
flicker and leap in solitary fires.
Tonight, this family's photos, viewed *in situ*,
invite replies. Here, in their preterite,
inviolate habitats, these privileged captives
present themselves as picnickers and bathers,
parishioners at leisure in their tweeds
and knickers, lovers on holiday. Their frail
and vanished souls retreat behind the mantel,
where shells lie still, and a matriarch presides.

4 Belfast in May

for Paul Muldoon

Off Donegall Square, the olive-colored gates
mock this island's undulating green.
Their ordered pikes jut upward into a sky
unmarked by bullet-pocks and unsurprised
by war. That neutral sky negotiates
a truce between things sacred and profane,
the blue-hazed hills and the Constabulary,
who scan the rainy shopping-mall, their eyes
scraping the scales from ordinary lives.
Better to be young than to remember
a linen city, prosperous and handsome.
Or better to be old and feel the throbs
less urgently, to view in cool perspectives
the yachts on the lough, the newsboy on the corner,
the bomb-hole's mouth. Or better to be numb
and smart, to congregate in drinking-clubs
and draw a festive screen across the trouble.
Visitor for a day, I speculate,
while those who live here burn their anthracite,
its fumes invisible, incivil, lethal.

Annaghmakerrig
Co. Monaghan, Ireland
May 1985

Small World

Better to take the measure
   of gaps and fissures
      than to venerate the wholes

that few of us believe in.
   Today, on the radio,
      in Cootehill, County Cavan,

Willie Nelson sings a sad
   and foreign song,
      his twang a counterpoint

to local brogues,
   his beat an ostinato
      to a lazy, rainy day.

Better to listen
   to a slow American tune
      while looking out on green

and yellow shopfronts,
   a Telefón booth with broken glass,
      a tired cyclist under his cap

making his way in the rain.
   Better to join, as best one can,
      a Texan's plaintive melody

with a fieldstone country church
   and breakfast-table talk
      of gelignite in Belfast.

Out of these quarried
   blocks of fact and memory
      may come a sturdy, small

indigenous shelter,
   its slate shingles holding out
      against hard weather.

Old Men of Monaghan

Is it rest they hanker for, or happiness,
those men who sip their stout in private corners?
Their canes sprawl on the carpet. Who knows where
they hide their griefs, or why they never married,
or what new slight will pester their remorse?
The publican ignores them. Something stirs
in the grate, as if its fall could goad the fire
out of its torpor. Better to leave them buried—
those angers that could smash the rusted locks
of disused cottages, those spites that heave
sharp stones at moss-grown walls. Above their heads,
the bottles make a judgment of their own
on all who elect regret for their mistakes
or speak in smoky parables that leave
the worst unsaid. What every conscience dreads
comes home at last, its song a monotone
beneath their breath, its shape an animal
that stains the corners of its squalid cage
with spittle and excrement, that vents its rage
on those who gawk or offer another meal.

Dublin in July

Mendacious Dublin, plying us with shades
of Yeats, Behan, Kavanagh, O'Brien,
inveigles us with drollery and squalor,
heroic ghosts transformed, transmogrified
by accident or craft. Remembered deeds,
remembered words, ennoble Pembroke Lane
and the rank corners of the Palace Bar.
See and believe? Beneath these deified
remains, the truth secretes itself. The silken
veil that half-conceals a marble face
proves, when touched, to be marble after all.
The document is false. The manuscript
purveyed as the original was written
more than once. Across from Percy Place
and down the weedy fringes of the Grand Canal
a light that is not angelic or corrupt
but strangely human, stretches its amber caul
over the bending trees and the filthy water.
The Georgian fanlight gleams above the door,
its panes effulgent and impenetrable.

1987

In Irishtown

He is taking her to task
on the front porch, their quarrel
travelling the sidewalk.

Embarrassed by his reddened
cheeks, his trembling jowls,
his whining accusations,

I make myself their judge,
their dumb apologist,
peeping through the haze,

deciphering the ragged
gestures of desperation,
the dialect of pain.

Stranger though I am,
I stop beyond the streetlight
and make myself at home—

a helpless, well-intentioned
healer in foreign dress,
calling at a house

where tainted clothes are burnt
and illness, being
human, has no cure.

Ogham

How could they be so old
and yet so ready, taking
into themselves the moment's
meanings, the shifting light
and the salty wind? Their lines
are the spirit's ladder, reaching
out of the stony soil
and the centuries' disorder.
Fish-skeletons of fact
and vain belief, they cherish
a chieftain's name, a local
victory, a passing.
Or (if it's true) a song,
a harpist's tablature.
Here are the riddles worn
on the stone's sleeve, the last
trace of a destination.
Beyond them, islands lost
to us and to themselves;
and here, the moment held
by a scrupulous notation,
not to be heard or known.

Dingle Peninsula
1986

Ante

We were believers then. The road
to the Methodist Church was lined with windows,
most of them friendly. Even the hard
pews provided sound advice;
the Good Shepherd dwelt in glass.

We brought our nickels into the schools,
swaddling them in handkerchiefs
or stuffing them deep in secret pockets.
And all our tradings in the alleys—
snake-eyes, shooters, cards—were a code

we understood. The carnivals
came with their hucksters swirling fire,
their gypsies fingering palms. Their voices
lassoed us into the tents; their fingers
pried at the faiths we'd locked inside.

And in the evenings, when our fathers
read from Deuteronomy
or dealt worn cards across the table,
we saw the kernels of ourselves
in the Jack's mask, the Joker's smile.

Mississippi Snappers

They were better left uncaught. They came
out of the river in dripping traps,
their armor muddy, their lizard-heads
covered with slime. All they could do

was harm. And when they lunged at us
through the wet ropes, we saw no fright
but only virulence in their eye-slits,
spite and defiance in their eyes.

Were we their jurors or their kin
in hiding? Taking them home, we saw
our inmost quarrels in the jaws
that fought our sticks, the hearts that beat

after dismemberment, the shells
hung up like shields on the market's walls.

Colloquy
for Gary Mensinger

On winter mornings the river broke
its vow of silence, grinding its ice
below the levee. What it said

was jagged, angular—a speech
unlike our own. We watched and listened,
finding in crushed floes, in rising

peaks of ice, a foreign lingo—
a dialect of collisions, thuds,
and low disturbances, a code

we could not decipher. Nor could our own
fragmented speech, our speechless breath,
paid out in arcs above the water,

answer the queries of cracking ice
or frame a letter in winter air.

Near the Solstice

The last I saw of him was in November,
a month for stacking wood and seeing off
the last few carriers of gratitude
and warmth, the changing seasons' winding train,
which takes its cargo over icy mountains
and meets its own reflection in the lakes
beyond our sight, the earth's blue apertures,

whose open pupils gather what we've known
or think we've known, enveloping the lost
or half-forgotten fact, the tattered story,
the memories that leave us when they must
and travel unaccompanied through landscapes
fit for the dead, their features still intact
but not for us, their voices unavailing.

Lament for the Holy Places

Once they were everywhere and held their candles
staunchly against the world's corrosive rime,
offering their wealth in small enclosures,
niches and shelters for the poor at heart,
who treated them with reverence or pity,
pausing to touch the carvings on a font,
or sign a register, or drop a coin

into a hollow box, whose velvet lining
gave back the resonance of things forgotten
or nearly so—the muted thud of silver
echoing through a nave or vestibule,
where insolence recoiled and silence lingered,
and darkness held its own against the glare
that broke through purple windows left ajar.

Fair Exchange
for Alexander

As he listened to my story
I saw, in his clear eyes, a son's
trust, a candle's

undeniable flame.
How radiant the room
became, each table edged

with filial light.
After the violence of doors
slammed, the darkness

of cold corridors at night,
this momentary gift
gave back the memory

of conscience still unscored
by hatred and remorse:
black earth before erosion.

Circlings
for Alexander

They are never really anecdotal,
those legends pilfered from childhood.
Anecdotes have endings. Tales

of setting a toilet seat on fire,
of pelting a squad car with tomatoes,
alter a little with each new telling,

till every kernel has been popped
or thrown away. The memory
that started it all, consumes itself,

leaving a picture of splattered metal,
flames in a bowl. And what it felt like
to be naïve, to play with matches,

to curse policemen from a tower,
is leaked away in laughs, or drained
in conversation. As for the story

of childhood itself, it seemed
to end—or have an ending. One
Saturday afternoon, a stranger's

voice took on a neutral tone
and all the worn diminutives—
Sonny, Bud, My Boy—sailed off

on a voyage of their own. And yet
to circumnavigate the globe
was not enough. They, too, came back,

appearing unexpectedly
in another father's reprimand
or praise, another son's horizon.

Swarming

Wherever they first began, those fears
of dogs and elevators swarmed
in the psyche, like the honeybees

we couldn't get rid of. Even the thought
of a German shepherd down the block
could change the direction of a walk,

as if those teeth, real or surmised,
had already sunk and left their scars
for good. As for that other fear,

it too could make the longer way
seem short. That bully with its cables,
its dreadful shaft, its sliding trapdoor

opening into the dark—who wouldn't
walk up seven flights of stairs
to dodge it? Maybe the worst convergence

would be to ride an antique lift
to the top floor, and there encounter,
behind stalled doors, two barking dogs.

That happened once. And in those long
nocturnal shafts we tumble into,
night after night, it will probably

recur. There is no smoke, no poison
to drive those squatters out, no way
to reap their combs, preserve their hives.

Sabula

You could carry the name *Sabula*
into this wintry landscape,
these bare maples chalked with snow,

and think its syllables exotic.
You could solemnly intone
its sounds against this rawness

of bark and ragged leaf
and think its little hillock
of consonant and vowel

a local promontory.
You could set aside the knowledge
you carry like your baggage—

the knowledge that Sabula
is a forlorn river town
passed over by the newsmen

flying to Chicago.
You could take that seed
and plant it, knowing your origins

for what they are, but wanting
the gaudy exotic flower
to spring from common soil

and the flag of poetry
to snap above the porches
of wide Midwestern houses.

Fiat Lux

for Ben and Rose Howard,
Ankeny, Iowa, c. 1933

One of the first: their lights came on
against a field they'd understood
only by daylight or swinging lantern.

What strangeness stirred them? Blades of light
from a loft awakened animals
that knew them only by their footfalls,

their heels on rock and gravel. Call it
Magic, or call it Moving Forward,
the message sang itself through darkness

into the mows and stalls. *You will*
be changed. Your cellars and your stairwells
will yield their privacies. Above

their roofs, a sky that never spoke
except in code, received their blessing,
their tungsten Host, their revelation.

For the Calvinists

They shaped their souls on anvils of righteousness
and their houses out of doctrinal regard
for things less tangible than hand-hewn beams,
wattle and oaken buckets, pewter cups,
or the brick-and-fanlight grandeur of the streets,
where a straitened elegance declared their faith

in a now-denuded sacrament of labor,
a reverence eroded by their waste,
their dream-fed greed and God-infected hunger,
its ghost discredited, its slow cortège
winding through neighborhoods and onto highways
made straight by destinies we can't remember.

Losing Ground

They lent me a certain trust, those lines you sent
in the mail—trust in the hunger of words to find
their ways, dependent a little, but not very much,
on us. At Gettysburg last year, I counted
gravestones the size of loaves. You could say the thousands
had been fed for good, their famous benediction

remembered when they are not. Poor words, allowed
to have their say, grown eloquent at last
because they were meet, because their contours fit
a country's sorrows and desires. You know
the story—how the other dignitary
talked for an hour that day, his noblest coinage

lost to posterity, to us. We wouldn't
like to be him up there, where now a marble
monument forgets whatever he said,
choosing instead the sentences whose current
flowed from necessity and pain. Most days
we ape that forgotten man, all bluster or mumble,

vanity or will. But once in a while
we trust the forms of things, however small,
to declare themselves in lattices of words,
arbors of metaphor. We name our daily
losses, knowing how slight they are beside
that field of stones, but no less real or final.

Reclamation

We can't relight their oil lamps
or turn the pages of their hymnbooks
with calloused hands, or recreate

the voice declaiming from the pulpit.
Tile by tile, their roof regains
its purity of line but not

its sanctity, its holy aura.
We can't believe what they believed
so earnestly, or deem their chapel's

Attic grace a sacrifice,
their pilasters a gift of love,
their hand-hewn weathervane a psalm.

That much is forfeiture. What rises
day by day from salvable
remains, from posts and antique beams,

invests itself in architraves
restored, in eaves rebuilt. We give
the gift of authenticity

as best we can, and summon truth
from nerves worn thin with irony
and self-protective gibes. New copper

fires their cupola and steeple,
as if to scare off loss or call
new faith from vacancies of clouds.

MacNeice at Ithaca, 1940

Not far from here, you made your peace with football,
praising the elegance of the forward pass
while finding shoulder pads ridiculous.
Little has changed, if you exclude our peculiar

wars of ovary and testicle,
the banishment of *lady*, *girl*, and *Miss*,
quarrels of *incuba* and *incubus*,
gender as melting point or point of honor.

You relished the leaping yells and somersaults
of the acrobatic cheerleaders (who were male)
and though your thoughts turned nervously to Hitler,
to Wavell's doggedness, or Chamberlain's

insipid reasoning, or Churchill's faults,
you heckled Syracuse and cheered Cornell.
This much has changed: tomorrow Leonard and Hagler
will settle a bitter score. We'll trade our pains

for ringside seats. With no more irony
than memory, we'll call their battle royal
a Bout to End All Bouts, a Super Duel,
or, if you like, the Fight of the Century.

1985

The world's long fires burn beyond
your window. You stir, arrange your pens,
write your notes to distant friends,
who hear—no less than you—the crash
of beams, the shouts and sirens. Brave

or cowardly, you want your friends
to answer for the violence
that rumbles under your pen, that shakes
your signature askew. The world's
black smoke has made a line you thought

your own, a hand you can't control
by will or diligent erasure.

Because You Asked for a Bedtime Story

The time will come when nothing of any worth
will be remembered by the connoisseurs
of video games, computers, frozen foods,
the whole warehouse going up in flames
or merely dissolving into molecules
of Western Culture, particles of value,
the atoms spinning freely into the void,

the center sliding, moment by moments, sideways
or into a darkness unrelieved by neon,
a formlessness we've dreamt of, after all,
though never seen, except in inferior films
or in those moments of our childhoods
when something shook the house, and no one came
to caress our brows and hasten us into sleep.

November

These last warm days are telling a funny story
whose punchline never comes. You could put your hand
on the iron railing of your neighbor's steps
and feel, in its frigid core, the steadiness
of winter. You could tell yourself the history
of winter's intransigence: the reprimand
contained in ice, the drainpipe's frozen lips,
the blocked reprieve. This last insouciance,
displaying itself in children chasing balls
into the street, in lazy tomcats curled
by the fence, in flights of blackbirds over the field,
speaks in the tones that everyone distrusts—
the timbre of laxity, the voice that counsels
ease and the thought of ease. The leaf unfurled
before it fell. The heart we thought was healed
gave out at sixty-nine. And now the crusts
strewn on the feeder whirl across the yard,
as though it were your office to provision
the appetites of chance, the hungry season,
or pay a debt that someone else incurred.

Lute Music

1 *Just Now*

That sudden impertinence
of crashing snow—the jolt
to the spine—recalls a moment
stranded in time: a March
morning in the country,
the dripping eaves, the hiss
of tires on the road.
For Wordsworth, memory
was nearly everything,
but here, among my brown
books and yellowing scores,
it seems that memory
is, at best, a candle
or, if you like, a lantern
held to the page. Forget
mistakes? Absolve the soul
in its own oblivion?
Out of that emptiness
there come the courtly dancers
of desire and regret,
to do their pirouettes,
their *pas de deux* among
the traces of *bourrées*
played by heart or rote,
and the thud of melting snow.

2 *Lute Music*

Lacking a common hymn
for Lent or Easter Sunday
I hear in the lute's divisions
an unmarked calendar—
days contained in quavers,

years in a phrase. And *Seven
Tears, Figured in Seven
Passionate Pavans*:
so the lute continues,
secular and courtly,
its inwrought counterpoint
inscribing curvatures
on emptiness, a black
absence, tracing maps
on a wilderness of silence.
Lacking a hymn for doubt
and louche uncertainties,
I hear in the lute's upheavals
the certainty of figures
remembering themselves
and watch, against a darkness
no longer thought divine,
those constellations brighten.

3 Elizabethan Dances

Tuned to itself and tuned
to a pitch beyond itself,
the lute restores a lush,
archaic harmony.
Relic of monarchies
and feudal innocence,
it hoards the figured forms
of allemande, pavane,
its voice a privileged cantor
chanting its own extinction.
Out of that ripened gourd
there grew a florid vine
too difficult to train
or prune, too plentiful
to manage. Not in shame
nor in the scarf and cane
of banishment and exile,

it left the world unmourned
by court or peasantry—
and now, in memory,
returns, its lineaments
refurbished by a hunch
or guess, its guttering candle
replenishing this room.

In the Regions of Belief

High voices sang. Those boys were strangers
to us and the congregation. Thorn
by thorn, I counted out the crown,
each point a pyramid of glass.

They were not for us, those otherworldly
valleys and peaks—that landscape made
of sound. It loomed outside our window,
distant and cold. We were its cautious

visitors, viewing each snow-laced ledge,
each foreign canyon through our own
reflections. Nothing would stop our train
from entering those centuries

again—or stop its passengers
from watching the ranges rise and fall,
the gorges lengthen into fields
we could not encompass or inhabit.

Lenten Anniversaries

Leafy-with-love banks and the green waters of the canal
Pouring redemption for me, that I do
The will of God, wallow in the habitual, the banal,
Grow with nature again as before I grew.

    PATRICK KAVANAGH

1

The noon siren sends its daily wail
over the snow-clogged streets, the white yards flecked
with tracks of cats, stray dogs, raccoons. It, too,
has made its mark on sheets of winter air,
its scrawls of black distress. If it should fail,
this delusive calm, which no one dares inspect
too closely, lest some snake come into view,
would be preserved, while somewhere, far or near,
bedrooms or silos would blacken in the sun.
How ludicrous, that such a signature
inscribed on a frigid sky, could sign away
decades of patient nurturing, a fretful
lifetime of planting and tending. One by one,
disfigured by fire or smothered by foreclosure,
or left to bed themselves in moldering hay,
the farms dispel the old belief. Regretful
witness, heir of a fruitful legacy,
I hear the thud of beams behind those calm
external walls, and wait for that alarm
to raise its flag of smoke in the winter sky.

2

This February cold conceals the flow
of currents and saps, of inadmissible thoughts
whose emblems rise in question marks of smoke
over the huddled houses. Only in dreams

do those forbidden griefs and angers show
their truant natures, thawing the mottled ruts
and loosening the grimace of the lake
until its stoic reticence, its claims
on virtue and truth, crack open at the center.
Now, in the daylight hours, walkers hurry
to classes and offices, their layers of scarves
binding them like bark. Should some desire,
licit or illicit, seek to enter
that unkempt, cold-water flat, where February
coughs in its sleep and stirs beneath its covers,
it would act the rapparee. Unwonted fire
would lap the edges of this purist's dream,
this holy metropolis, where rectitude
parades in rigid streams and frozen blood,
and the ghost of lust retreats, a forgotten crime.

3

We waken daily to the reprimands
of jays, the sash's gavel. Lengthening days
invade the nights' fantasias, where rubato
slackens the rules. The stricter disciplines
of morning showers, chores, impending errands,
purge the spirit of its formless ways,
and fashion, out of clay, a shrewd mulatto
who bears the pigment of his dreams, the stains
of deviance, the apostatic scars.
Impenitent, heretical, he makes
the awkward motions that the day requires,
and finds in February's grays and browns,
in pockmarked avenues and muddied doors,
a mirror for his barters and mistakes,
his necessary lies. When his desires
compose a melody without a ground,
an oratorio without a fable,
he fabricates a plot, a parable,
an improvised libretto from the daily round.

4

Thawing, the drifts concede their character;
the etched channels blur. This harsh effacement
topples their features into heaps of slush,
mounds of gratuitous remains. To yield
identity so pliantly, to stare
so equably at oblivion or torment,
is a grace denied to us, who loathe the rush
of years, who crave a marker in the field,
a plaque, an epitaph. Today the airmen
killed overseas in nineteen seventy-three
came back in shards, while veterans made peace
on Iwo Jima. Provisional or final,
those rituals and gestures toward reunion
call up the clackings in Ezekiel's valley,
echoes of requiem and Easter service.
In downtown shops, the spirit's seasonal
renewal clothes itself in Easter suits,
in showy retinues of summer cotton,
or mutes its own ebullience in lenten
articles, in abstinent blues and whites.

5

Behind their thickening reddish haze, the maples
relinquish definition. How often love
of opulence and love of the austere
open and close a shutter on the world,
a creaking hinge. Today some obscure scruples
forbid the excursion of a morning drive
on muddy roads; some fear of the impure
denies a digressive walk, an untoward
adventure. Out of my sight, the elms' unfinished
scores acquire a few new notes; the pines
construct new chords within the old constraints.
And out of my control, the appetites
of memory break their fasts, their stores replenished

with resonant sentences, enduring scenes.
In one, a minister voices his complaints,
his faith in grace. The congregation sits,
stern and reserved. It's Easter and it's spring,
or nearly so. The pure extravagance
of altar lilies, their wild intemperance,
tug at the service's restraining string.

    6

In flooded cornfields last year's broken stalks
flutter and oscillate, their history
almost complete. Spirit of nascent thought,
your creatures swarm beneath that glassy surface;
your force harrows the air. If you should coax
hard meanings from the world's uncertainty,
those sturdy innocents might germinate
some untold leaf or mutant synthesis.
Today my forty years have watched their damp
revenants rise from mounds of khaki grass
and hover in low clouds above the highway.
Drive on, they seem to say; and west of here,
their cellars filling, families decamp
to makeshift shelters while their goods disperse.
Their privacy invaded by a fluent clay,
their lineages subsumed by shapeless water,
they will live in faceless dwellings for a while,
until their remnants can be cleansed of silt,
their vestiges restored, their faith rebuilt.
Said one: "We tried to stop it with a towel."

7

Consensus gentium? At Hiroshima,
the split atom broke that wholesome code.
And here the snow returns in particles,
discrete as sects or clans. This morning, March
snorts at the gate, an unregenerate Brahma,
ready to toss off riders, churn up mud,
and dash all schemes aside. Old articles
of faith, old certitudes, will feel the lurch,
the kicking and commotion. Now the dream
of wholeness steadies itself in frozen creeks,
in crusts and ridges. Beneath that dream, the surge
of memory hurries stories, chunks of gossip,
imaginings and portents into a time
as yet unknown. Should those unorthodox,
unseemly fragments finally converge
in stark tableaux and attitudes of worship,
their frigid witnesses will stand on water.
Their hope will be a floating Boniface,
their charity a crèche of melting ice,
their faith an arctic shelter ringed by fire.

Alfred, New York
February-March 1985

On Reading Some of My Poems
for Harry Duncan

How often they look backward,
those melancholy lines,
finding in Irish towns
and Pennsylvania fields
their truest register.
Surely you understand
that hankering for lost
or forlorn courtesies,
that thirst for civility.
Is that what inveigles us,
time and again, to write
and print what can't survive
indifference, neglect,
and quick remaindering?
How often they surprise me,
those lines on antiquated
buildings and battlefields,
not with their elegiac,
fastidious detachment,
nor yet with their contingent
of undefined regret,
but with their outcry, guised
as chronic retrospection.
Call it an obbligato
or *basso continuo*,
that muted indignation.
Surely you recognize
its slow, insistent voice
urging, against the force
of elegiac longing,
a venturesome rebuttal
or, as the case may warrant,
a truculent survival.

Midcentury

(1997)

I

The Word from Dublin, 1944

I greet you from a neutral country in a neutral hour.
　　ROBERT GREACEN

The neutral island in the heart of man.
　　LOUIS MACNEICE

I

I can't begin to say what brought me here,
Unless it be the Irish predilections
For whiskey and horses, both of which entail
A certain risk and a less-than-certain gain.
To be a middle-aged American
In Dublin in the middle of a war,
Of which we're hearing more or less than nothing,
And that in fragments, bits of veracity—
A mutilated bulletin, a headline—
Is to see one's lot reflected in the stories
That come to us distorted, if at all:
Stories of heroism, sacrifice,
Or, more often, utter devastation.
Of Irish horses I know next to nothing.
Of Irish whiskey I can claim the knowledge
Given to those who can't pretend to know
The subtle processes of distillation
By which a grain becomes a thing of beauty
And a *force majeure* in decimated lives
But know too well the amber Irish jewel
That shoots its radiance though heart and soul
And soothes the brains it hastens to dismantle.
Water of life indeed—its irrigation
Useful to a spirit somewhat parched

By human frailties and human needs
Or, more specifically, the final exit
Of her whom I was pleased to call my wife
Until I called it quits and left those scenes
Of mutual defeat and exploitation
And she, in concert, left for Colorado,
Taking her parrots and our only child.
Or, more recently, my troubled lover,
Savagely beautiful but off her rocker,
Who also bolted, taking neither child
Nor furniture but much of my belief
In sanctity and high-romantic logic.
Reasons enough to sojourn in a country
Notorious for its hospitality,
Itself no stranger to intestine wars
But neutral where the lunacies of Hitler
And the blusterings of Churchill are concerned—
And to find some consolation in a landscape
Which in the evenings sometimes calls to mind
The saintly scholar's tranquil countenance
Or, if you like, the monks at Clonmacnoise
Transcribing psalms and jotting marginalia
In perfect peace, before the Danes' arrival.

II

The heart has many corners, but this city
Is, I think, a diagram of corners,
Not least the pungent snugs of the Palace Bar,
Those corners where the heart can talk itself
Out of its misery or celebrate
Its minor triumphs over a ball of malt.
That last is Irish for a shot of whiskey,
A phrase I fancy only a little less
Than the thing itself, mainly because it captures
The truth about the permanence of things.
For what that trick of speech is calling solid
Is really liquid, not precisely formless

But certainly susceptible to change,
By which I mean consumption, disappearance.
On that one point, if nowhere else, the Irish
Remind me of those smiling Buddhist monks
Who make impermanence their daily meditation,
Along with suffering, the formless ego,
And the spectacle of loved ones' flesh decaying.
For death, as the poet said, is never far
From the Irish mind, or ever very far
From the darker corners of the Palace Bar,
Where sometimes in the evenings I allow
My thought to circulate around my father,
That stout Midwestern Methodist, whose leading
Scruple was a stern sobriety
In talk as well as drink. *Weigh your words*,
He told me—sound advice, if seldom taken,
And seldom needed, now that certain words
Carry more weight than anyone can manage.
'What's eating *them?*' I asked my sober sister,
Noticing, off to the side, two upright farmers
Standing at attention like those Gothic
Oldsters in the painting. 'Don't you know,'
My sister said, 'They have *moralysis.*'
That was a dream, some thirty years ago.
I *didn't* know. How *could* I, having grown
Almost to manhood with that same affliction,
Which causes Iowans to see the world
As more coherent than it really is
And gamely to construct a moral dream
Where black is black, and a promise is a promise?
In the nether corners of the Palace Bar,
Where black is seldom black, or a fact a fact,
My father's dream can seem a kind of madness.
And just to keep my bearings in this country,
Whose ancient language has no words for Yes
Or No, but only subtle shades of meaning,
I sometimes scratch the facts on sodden napkins:
I'm forty-eight. My son is nine. Tonight
Is June twenty-second, nineteen forty-four.

V

Let me define a word for you: *erasure*.
Its root, *radere*, means to *scrape*; its prefix,
E, means *out*. Hence, *a scraping out*.
Its closest synonyms—*efface, expunge,
Delete, cancel*, and *obliterate*—
Approximate its meaning but miss out
Its modern connotations: blackboards, sponges,
A gentle rubbing, leaving a trace or smear
Indicative of error, misdirection,
A change of mind, a wise reversal. Once
On Kildare Street, on a Thursday afternoon,
As I made my way to the National Museum,
Clicking the black gate that separates
Irish antiquities from Irish streets,
I shuddered—not out of pity or regret
Or anything so noble as respect,
But out of a sudden sympathy for myself,
Remembering, as I did, those multiple
Erasures. Youth and faith. My daffy lover . . .
A senile mother, speaking words aloud . . .
Luckily for me, I snapped myself
Out of that bootless fit of self-absorption
And took my tour of the National Museum,
Viewing erasure on a larger scale,
By which I mean the ruthless, systematic
And mere erasure of the Gaelic order.
Necklaces and bracelets, pendants, rings,
The Ardagh Chalice and the Tara Brooch—
Those relics only underscored the sad
Finality, the pathos of it all.
I told you so, a parrot might have said
To Hugh O'Neill at the Battle of Kinsale,
That armature on which a culture swivelled,
Gathered speed, and spun into extinction.
And again *I told you so* to those ripe souls,
The self-made martyrs of the Easter Rising.
Their letters, uniforms, and diaries,

Their tiny pistols raised against an empire—
What lesson there, except it be the lesson
That wild courage, careless of its losses,
Can teach the rest of us—we cautious ones,
Who know too much, or have too much to lose?
I moralise, I know. I have no right.
But just the other night at the Palace Bar,
I heard the tale of the O'Rahilly,
Mortally wounded in the insurrection,
Who dipped his finger in his own life's blood
And daubed his R.I.P. on a Dublin doorstep.
'Now *there's* presence of mind,' my inner cynic
Started to say—until my inner critic
Rebuked him harshly for his glib remark.
And then my heart, pumping itself for combat,
Offered the less-than-startling observation
That truth and courage drink from a common well.
And last, my judgment, having the final say,
Reminded all of us that youthful men,
Dying without regret for their beliefs,
Are not more foolish than the spectacle
Of unbelieving sods in drafty tweeds
Sipping their whiskeys and their pints of Guinness.

VI

    Call it the light of things awakening
In late July, the light on water trembling
Beneath the overpass, the furtive light
That is no younger than the crumbling stone
But nonetheless deceives you into seeing,
In water splashing rock, in water threading
A path through channels smaller than your hand,
A ghost of youth, a phantom of renewal.
Whatever it is, it's come belatedly
To me, as to this neutral, youthful nation,
Which after two millennia may yet
Bestir itself from De Valera's dream
Of purity and perfect isolation
And find, despite its national inertia,
Its place among the nations of the world.
If what we've heard from Normandy is true
The world may soon have cause for celebration,
If also cause for vengeance, cause for mourning.
As for me, I spend my waking hours
Compiling the unlikeliest of books,
An Irish lexicon, and writing long
Inconsequential stories for my son,
Who, if anyone, can still be neutral
And still believe in leprechauns and fairies.
And sometimes when the sun is coming up
I look out on the waters of the bay
And dream of drifting mines, and count my blessings,
And measure my success in Irish miles.

II

Stone on Stone
Dingle Peninsula, 1945

> *We are all now dispossessed.*
> PAUL MULDOON

I

    I wonder whether poverty or water
Is more to be feared—the first so dangerous
To health and happiness, the second likely
To drown our sorrows with the rest of us
And leave our children permanently poor.
After a hampered year in Dublin City
I've settled here—a foreigner as always
But certainly no stranger to the sound
Of water splashing in a whiskey glass
And water supping freely on the rocks
Fronting the wild sea at Dunbeg Fort,
Which are to all appearances removed
From any danger of impermanence
But are, when all is said, as vulnerable
As you or I to gradual extinction.
It wasn't innocence that prompted me
To rent this house in Ballyferriter
And so remove myself from urban noises
And urban pleasures—innocence, that is
Of human tricks and natural disasters.
Call it a hunger. Or call it something old
And spacious in the basement of the psyche,
A recreation room where fallen gods
And nascent hankerings disport themselves
In motley colours, blathering all the while
Of purity and imminent renewal.
To that perennial recuperation
This place could be the answering refrain,

Itself a stomping-ground, an injured party
With fifty centuries of habitation
Under its belt and more than one defeat
To test its fortitude and call its own.
A little short of cash but long on relics,
It lives on memory, as some of us
Subsist on lust, or thrive on desolation.

II

How did it happen that the two of us
Fell out, our bodies seeking private quarters,
Our spirits separate retreats? Not
The best of friends, we nonetheless remained
For all intents and purposes a marriage,
Founded not in Heaven nor in Hell
Nor in the cruelties of youthful passion,
But in the mutualities and causes,
Common or otherwise, that make dependents
Out of the most unfriendly nation-states
And from the brass of sheer necessity
Fashion a leash, or forge a brazen chain.
I was her father, she my surrogate mother.
I was her innocent, her new arrival,
Stuffing her vacant nest but less than pleased
To draw my breath beneath that pile of feathers.
Thus our analyst explained the case,
Fighting, I thought, bewilderment and boredom.
And in the end his costly clarities,
Such as they were, availed us very little
And were as nothing next to broken glass,
The sucker punches, mostly below the belt,
The savage insults, never to be forgotten.
Following custom more than inclination,
I packed my bags—and thus became the latest
Volunteer in that uncomely legion,
The regiment of fathers dispossessed
Of hearth and armchair, dignity and stature.
Watching the waves at Ballydavid pier
I think of nothing—nothing except the night

I came as stranger to my own front porch,
Wearing the mantle of the absent father.
Better to think of nothing than to dwell
Too long on that abrupt humiliation
Or see again my child's frightened eyes
Watching behind his mother's flaring skirt—
Or hear again the crashing of that door
With all the vengeance of her grief behind it
And all the solemn majesty of the law.

IV

And now the strangeness of the days advances,
Not in a rush but with a steadiness
That rattles me—as once the river's water,
Dropping beneath the weight of my canoe,
Awakened fears I'd rather not remember.
That happened of a summer afternoon
Some thirty years ago—a nice surprise
For one whose innocence was still inherent
And who for all his brooding had no clue
To the certainties of loss and deprivation.
Watching that early version of myself
In memory, I scarcely recognize
The silly kid who blundered into Lock
And Dam 13 on the Mississippi River
And felt the water like an elevator
Lower itself and him with no more warning
Than might be granted to an alcoholic
Just on the brink of scotching wife and child
Or some incorrigible adulterer
Undoing love with the dialing of a number.
Here on an island's bleak extremity,
My son and I a hemisphere apart,
I feel again that blank, enormous wall
Banging against the hull of my canoe
And the slime-hung rope by which I held my own,
The water draining steadily beneath me,
As down a shaft or foul-smelling hole.
It was, I think, my earliest intimation

Of sudden loss and self-inflicted wounding,
Of which all later acts of dispossession,
Sudden or gradual, imposed or chosen,
Were but a clear and rueful confirmation.

V

There is a bitter, eremitic joy,
Grounded not in touch or conversation
Or in the colloquies of loving friends
But in the sure repose of sand and stone
And the poverty of silent contemplation.
Hardly the one to munch on watercress
And chant myself to sleep between cold stones,
I tip my hat to those intransigents,
Those wily Gaels and self-negating monks,
Who could have given in but chose instead
To build their huts in this forsaken place,
Their little beehive huts, devoid of bees
But swarming with their vows and abnegations.
Theirs was not a militant resistance,
And the preservation of their Oratory—
So vulnerable to storms and demolitions—
May be a happenstance, a stroke of luck,
A baffling oversight of Cromwell's armies.
Nevertheless, I find in their condition
An emblem of my own, and in their chapel
A mentor for my unbelieving mind.
Certain of very little, I'm convinced
That memory itself is mortarless,
Its elements no larger than a hand,
Its hut a curvature of jointless stones.
Lost in the nestings of my monkish bed,
I relish, now and then, those ruptured stones,
Which are, when all is done, my true possessions,
Crude as they are by ordinary standards,
Dark as they are by ordinary light.

III

The Mother Tongue
Co. Kerry, 1946

> *I am accustomed to their lack of breath . . .*
>   W. B. Yeats

I

With not a word of Irish to my name
And no more purpose than befits a maker
Of etymologies and definitions,
I've brought my books and papers to this place,
Where field and furrow speak in Irish phrases
And English is at best an afterthought,
At worst a numb and merciless invader,
Who saw his own reflection in the landscape
And left no word or name inviolate.
Across the water, more than one invader
Has left the field, discovered suicide,
Or heard at Nuremburg the final word
On genocide and brute imperial power.
But here in County Kerry, English words
And English names perpetuate a story
Retold at every cottager's expense
And written in the bent, bilingual signs
Which take it as their mission to mislead
The traveller, or otherwise impede
The next imperialist, the next invader.
And underneath the skewed phonetic spellings,
The conqueror's confused approximations,
There runs a speech as fluent as the feeling
Of loss itself—a feeling not unknown
To a forty-nine-year-old American
Whose recent history has more in common
With a long bout of Spanish influenza

Than with the confidence of British voices
Intoning plaudits over their pile of rubble.
Another harmless drudge, I hear my fortunes
Echoed not in Standard English timbres
But in the rise and fall of Irish voices,
The earthy consonants and liquid vowels,
The supple and mysterious ellipses
Of a tongue that has for centuries lamented
Its banishment to zones of stony soil,
And fashioned out of memory and pity
A parable of ruth and Gaelic glory.

II

    What is a mother tongue if not a vessel,
Impervious to rain but vulnerable
To ruin? Here in the Gaeltacht, smashed and scattered
Over the rocky fields of western counties,
The mother tongue resembles nothing more
Than bits and pieces of an ancient vase,
Whose sturdy clay reliably contained
The truths of saga, balladry, and song,
The cold ferocity of poets' curses,
The seacoast dirges and the *sean-nós* cries
And crazy Sweeney warbling in his tree.
And though each shard retain the history
And half-remembered grandeur of the whole,
The whole has vanished into empty air,
Condensing here and there in mound or dolmen,
In passage-graves and rings of standing stones.
But while I'm thinking of the mother tongue
I can't help adding that apostrophe
Which bears the freight and onus of possession
And makes the mother tongue a mother's tongue—
That tablespoon and weapon of destruction,
So fit for nurturing or rendering,
For feeding open minds and trusting eyes
Or ripping infant psyches, limb from limb.

All of this by way of introducing
That savage moment from my childhood
When Mother, having heard of my affection,
My childish crush on someone else's daughter,
And having heard from me the prototype
Of all my later lovesick declarations,
Retailed my story to her next-door neighbours
And spilled my innocent, untried desires
Over the coffee cups and playing cards,
The chocolate wafers and the word Canasta.
In a small corner of that living room,
Recoiling from the blow of that explosion,
I listened to the voice of an announcer
And heard in low, authoritative tones
That I could be sure if it was Westinghouse.
For a long time, I curled up on a cushion
Repeating that insinuating phrase.
But decades on, I'm sure of very little,
Except that in the passing of a moment
And the passing of my words across the table,
I learned the bitter truth of violation,
The first invasion of the private heart,
And learned against a child's deepest wish
That I could love but never trust my mother.
Walking the sandy beach at Brandon Bay,
Its warmth a solace to my calloused feet,
I call upon those waters to remove
The last contusions of that primal hurt
And speak across an arc of forty years
The words of peace and the phrases of forgiveness.

IV

    Mother was not the sort to magnify
My failings, gross as they were, and not the one
To punish me overtly or directly
For sins against the gods of Common Sense
And the deities of Reasonable Behaviour.
Her *modus* was a tacit disapproval,
A dexterous and lateral manoeuvre
By which the ball of wax was deftly passed
Across to its creator, namely me.
Putting my drab supper on the table,
Her back bent in a posture of submission,
She dished out more than meat and mashed potatoes.
'It's *your* funeral,' she liked to say,
Enforcing by that apt exaggeration
The scruples of a Methodist, who fancies
Himself the cause of each abomination
That comes his way, and keens himself to sleep
On misplaced griefs and sorrows not his own.
Every now and then, I think of her
Mopping the floor and muttering her contempt
For fops and wastrels, hypocrites and fools.
But what was I thinking of that afternoon,
Driving through the precincts of Listowel,
The weather not the best for making choices,
The rain a subtle register of doubt?
Cursing the rain, I parked my borrowed car
In the town square, facing the iron gate
And the iron palings, black as any frock,
That kept their sober church apart from traffic.
And then I left, returning hours later
To find my car mysteriously surrounded
By other cars, my exit blocked entirely.
Uncanny is the word for what prevailed
That afternoon—a close, uncanny silence,
Where no one spoke or ambled through the square
And the soft rain sustained an atmosphere
Of penitential grief and absolution.

Was it the weather or the silent men
Who slouched outside the pub, their caps and coats
Dampening in the rain? Or was it I,
Who summoned up the mourner in myself
And left the dry interior of my car
To stand among some others in the square,
Folding my arms, as if to watch a race,
Or hear a speech, or judge a boxing match?
After a time, undoing all pretense
Of knowing where I stood or what I stood for,
I asked a *garda* what was going on.
'A funeral,' he said. 'A mother of nine.'
And then we chatted for a little while,
Exchanging pleasantries and anecdotes,
And fending off the presence of the mother,
Whose coffin had already come to light
And now was winding through the open gate,
Borne on the shoulders of her son, her brother,
And others whom the *garda* could have listed—
They and their families, for generations.
Seldom have I felt more fraudulent
Or more in violation of the codes,
The histories and shibboleths that bind
A parish to an image of itself,
A culture to its own reclusive centre.
Unwitting, well-intentioned, inadvertent—
Was I not the latest incarnation
In a long line of ignorant invaders,
Meeting the Irish on their own terrain?
It was not my funeral and never would be,
Though what I saw of foreign lamentation
And foreign tears collapsed all definitions—
Their grief my grief, their lineaments my own.

V

O holy longing. Not the turn of phrase
To please a querulous apostate. Not
A sentiment to generate belief
From one who had the calling to dismantle
Those articles of faith on which his rocker
Lifted and dipped—those wicker certainties
On which he'd sat, thinking himself complete.
'Too serious by half,' the lady said,
Herself unburdened by those borrowed griefs
And rented grievances which sometimes drive
My conscience into alien terrain.
But once again, the lady was mistaken.
Solemn as I can be, and sometimes am,
I've seldom shown the seriousness that questions
Its own proclivity to questioning
And entertains, if only for a moment,
Its gravest hints and holiest of longings.
Such is my regret this Sunday morning,
The weather rueful even by Irish standards,
The damp parishioners in hats and scarves,
Their faces redolent with absolutes,
Leaving their place of sanctity and worship.
We hew and delve, but when it comes to matters
Too intimate for rational dispute,
I fear the virulence of definitions,
The intellect's unsparing violations.
Beyond this island, nursing their ghoulish wounds,
The nation-states adjust their boundaries,
Composing polities and mapping bridges
Over disparities of race and creed
And making out of multiple invasions
A not-so-just and not-so-stable order.
Hearing the tongues of bells proclaiming peace
Over an increment of Irish rain,
I ask myself how often I've invaded
The sanctities I scarcely understand
And by the analyst's inquiring hand

Done harm without and violence within.
What is a grievous loss if not the faiths
Of childhood invaded by the knives
And needles of the sceptical adult,
Who has, for all his self-condoned intentions,
Divided soul from body, heart from mind,
And left himself bereft of his address
Or any promise of a lasting home?
Ochone! Ochone! for those unruly phantoms,
Those fantasies of innocence and order,
Which even now accompany the sight
Of narrow streets and fractured paving-stones
And foreign recusants returning home.

IV

Spitting Forgiven
Dublin, 1947

> *After such knowledge, what forgiveness?*
>   T.S. ELIOT

> I have you, and I'm more than grateful to
> you. But sure I'd expect no less from you.
> You're all nature.
>   BRENDAN BEHAN—*The Quare Fellow*

I

Having a staunch affection for this city,
Where gas was rationed not so long ago
And brewing a cup of tea at certain hours
Was tantamount to brewing bootleg whiskey,
I've spent a winter in a furnished flat
Just north of Sandymount, my whiskey warmed
By water from a steaming, legal kettle.
So many laws were broken by the tanks
And bayonets of troops across the water,
It seems a piece of moral sophistry
That here in Ireland a pensioner
Could find his pension nicked, his honour dented,
For heating a little water on the sly—
Or, as the Dubs would have it, *on the glimmer*.
Grey bread, grey paper, hoarded food and petrol,
The ration-books that told us *There's a war on*,
Have vanished with the coming of the English,
The young Parisians strolling Nassau Street,
The menus in the window of the Gresham,
Which give the passing tourists the impression
Of enviable prosperity and calm.

What lingers from the old austerity
And catches my professional attention
Is not so much the relics as the phrases
Which have a life and vector of their own.
To be a Yankee lexicographer
Among the Irish is to have one's ears
Bombarded with the likes of *hoor* and *stocious*,
Which have their share of meaning for the talkers
Who occupy the benches on the green
But have no home in any lexicon
And leave a Yankee's thirst for definition
Unsatisfied, his palate teased and thwarted.
With not enough to show for fifty years
And plenty to remember and regret,
That's not the only hunger I've brought with me
To Ireland—this home for desperadoes,
Who've lived for several centuries on the glimmer
And seem, at times, to savour desperation.
Just yesterday a Dubliner informed me
That a *glimmer* was a residue of gas
Left in the pipes, after the valves were closed—
Enough to brew a pot but not enough
To cook a meal or heat a clammy home.
And at the door, at any time, could come
The glimmer man   the dour Gas Inspector,
Checking the jets for signs of indiscretion.
With all such practices and deprivations
I feel a certain mutuality,
Having myself subsisted on the whiffs
Of old theologies, and having lived
For decades in a state of disapproval,
Of moral dread and imminent remonstrance,
As though the spirit's fuel were illicit
And the *Glimmer Man* were just around the corner.

III

    What is the name for that capaciousness
Which duly notes a drunkard's thickened speech
And sees a lecher wheeling out of orbit
And hears a liar's mangling of the facts
But still extends its welcome to the culprit
And offers a warm seat beside the fire?
Here in Ireland they call it *nature*,
By which they mean no pastoral seclusion
But quite the opposite—a gross immersion
In human messiness and imperfection,
The oversights that botch the perfect wedding,
The phones that seldom work, the clocks that can't
Agree or tell the truth, the mail that has
A will of its own, arriving when it pleases.
And, beyond all that, the brutal failings,
The dark malignities. Walking the beach
At Bray, my heels unsteady in the sand,
My beard regaled by another Irish drizzle,
I thought of the little signs on Dublin trams
Declaring their improbable proscription.
Spitting forbidden, they warn the traveller,
As though the smoker's most forbidding habit
Were more containable than Irish rain—
Or less promiscuous than human malice,
Which drops its parcels, when and where it chooses.
Would that all those mailings might be gathered
Into a carton marked *Return to Sender*.
And would that all the spittings of those madmen
Who called themselves *il Duce* and *der Führer*
Had been forbidden by some higher power
Before their virulence became endemic,
Their spittle lethal. Tale by horrid tale,
The stories of the massacres and death trains,
The images of wholesale executions,
The testaments of skeletal survivors,
Have made their way through folds of insulation
And have, for some of us, assumed the stature

Of household gods and secular mementoes,
Reminding us—even at this remove—
Of moral voids and unforgivable evil.
Yet even as I say that, I'm recalling
An evening spent in Ennis, County Clare,
The lights low in a dusky music hall,
The *sean-nós* singers weaving their plaintive stories
Of sons and fathers lost, of families
Destroyed by waves and fatal human choices.
Strange as it may seem, what caught my notice
And stirred some dormant knowledge in my blood
Was not so much the singers' nasal voices,
Their liquid trills and miniature cadenzas
But what erupted from their audience—
Or, if I may steal a forlorn word
Out of my childhood, their *congregation*.
Indigenous and mostly in their fifties,
Their faces grooved, their eyes exuberant,
They knew the words and melodies by heart.
And when their voices joined the choruses
An octave lower, reminding me of thunder,
It seemed the voice of some volcanic passion
Contained in stone—the voice of suffering,
Replete with grief and cognizant of anguish.
It was—or so I thought—the voice of *nature*,
Forgiving fate and fatal human error—
Or the voice of humankind forgiving God
For each new loss, each bloated casualty.

IV

My father held his own behind a curtain
Of reticence and patient understanding—
Not the sort of curtain one could part
Without an effort, a yanking at the cords,
A noticeable friction in the pulleys,
A stopping-short. And I was not the one
To crawl beneath those folds of crumpled velvet

Where no one, even I, had been invited.
In that respect, I was my father's child,
Preserving someone else's privacy
As though it were an article made sacred
By years of awe and silent veneration.
Odd that my father's voice should come to mind
Just as I was crossing Nassau Street,
Thinking not of Methodists or silence,
Much less a Methodist's unnerving calm,
But of the etymology of *stern*,
Its roots in *star* and Viking fortitude.
Odd that in the din of cars and lorries
A son should hear a voice entirely vanished
Except in memory and meditation—
A stern but melancholy baritone,
Judicious to a fault, but not without
The registers of tenderness and sorrow.
Odder still that as I made my way
Around the curve of Grafton Street,
What should present itself but something risen
Out of the ashcan of my childhood,
As if to admonish me or call me home.
But there I was, alone, before my father's
Office door, its window painted black.
And there, against that interstellar void,
Its ten injunctions framed in red and gold,
Its code set down in gilded Roman letters,
Was nothing milder than the Decalogue—
My father's notion of a welcome mat,
Greeting me with its promise of remorse
For stolen dimes and nickels, mindless pranks,
The daily mischiefs of a nine-year-old
Who took the Ten Commandments seriously
But often failed to mention his misdeeds

And sometimes framed them, even to himself,
As accidents or trivial moral blunders,
Better to be forgotten than reproved.
It wasn't long before the blare of traffic
And the jostlings of the shoppers on the sidewalk
Undid my reverie and ushered me
Back to the slanted light of Grafton Street.
But what that moment's vision left me with
Comes back to me in dreams, as though that blackness
Were not a curtain but the man himself
And the ten Reminders posted on his window
Were the features of the ghost who fathered me
And to this day reminds me of my failings,
Even as he guides me down a sidewalk
Littered with coins and scraps of foreign paper.

VI

    Something possessed me of a Friday morning
To ride the bus from Dublin to Armagh,
Leaving, as it were, the seat of commerce
For the brain of temporal authority
And the bald head of patriarchal power.
Watching the shifting light above the drumlins
And the stony fields of County Monaghan,
I felt a darkening within myself
And in that megalithic Northern landscape,
As though a voice were deepening by the mile.
And after that, Armagh, its apple orchards
Sifting the chaff of amber Northern light.
Eden it was not, but looking out
On the stands of apple trees, their well-pruned branches
Heavy with ripened fruit, I sensed the presence
Of innocence and imminent fulfilment.
Beyond the orchards came the town itself,
Its newly painted shops, its sudden hills,
And on my left and right, its twin cathedrals,
Catholic and Protestant, respectively.

Around the latter one, some scaffolding
Signified attention and renewal—
Or, if you like, a vote for preservation.
Watching a scruffy mason pointing stonework,
A workman hauling buckets up a ladder,
I thought of other schemes and restorations
And what's been going on across the water—
The bombed-out cities picking up the pieces,
The nation-states arising out of rubble.
Returning home, I called to mind a dream
I've had not once, but often: myself out walking
In shorts or wraps, depending on the weather,
The field before me overgrown with weeds,
And my own steps uncertain. And then a room,
A chamber, rather. The smell of plaster dust.
The taps of mallets in a vacant choir.
And overhead, a net of ribs and bosses
From which the graven faces frown and smile.
Misericordias, or some such motto,
Allures me to a solitary corner,
And there, amidst a momentary whiteness,
An ambience of faith without an altar,
I recognize that fabric as my own.
Call it a half-built temple or cathedral,
Or something yet to be identified
And yet to shed its light upon its maker.
Spitting forgiven, I would have them mount
Over the door of the confessional—
Or better yet, the meditation hall,
Where once a day I'd take my threads of malice,
My coiled dreads and animosities,
My mother's angers and my father's laws.
And there, beneath a window left ajar,
I'd watch those knots unravel in the languors
Of late afternoon, as though the force of *nature*
Had caused their old solidities to vanish,
Their rancours to dissolve in liquid light.

V

The Center of Attention
Co. Monaghan, 1948

I

   Across the water it was called the War,
But here in Ireland, where parachutes
Redeemed from wreckages were resurrected
As silken blouses, silken skirts and scarves,
The Irish called it the Emergency,
At once reducing its significance
And lending to the gists of common things—
To tillage, turf, paper, bread, and petrol—
A patina of worth and urgency.
It's all in how you see it, I suppose,
But after half a decade in this country
I've come to wonder if my way of seeing
Is not as fixed as that of Irish farmers,
Their backs to the Atlantic and their eyes
Converging on the coulter and the furrow.
What motive did I have in coming here
Except to make a book of roots and meanings,
A small, Hiberno-English lexicon,
And in the process find a little solace,
A welcome respite from those urgencies
Which might be called, for lack of better words,
My private War, my soul's Emergency?
How fitting that a lexicographer
Of modest birth and dubious distinction
Should bring his woes and homely pigeon-holes
To an island that eludes all definitions
And seek relief from chronic self-delusion
In an ambience where passions and obsessions
Are not so much exceptions as the rule.
Five years on, I've made but little progress

On either project, having nothing more
To show for all my efforts than a heart
As prone as always to befuddlement
And stacks of scribbled notes, as yet unordered
And less than lucid, even to their author.
What better mirror for a bungled life
Than sheaves of synonyms and antonyms
Recorded with meticulous precision
But written in a hand unduly fine—
A pile of useful, useless information
Which grows a little deeper by the day
And which, if I should die before I wake,
Will be at best a present for my son,
A tribute to his father's misdirection,
A monument to scholarly attention
At odds with chaos and the rush of time.

II

Where did it begin, that cast of mind
Which sets its painted idol at the centre
Of each new circumstance? Which wrenches each
New thought into a vector of devotion
And spurs the votary to squander hours
And dollars in the service of a mistress
Who will, if true to form, abandon him,
Withdrawing by that act the very rug
On which he paid preposterous obeisance?
I'm sure that if I knew, I've since forgotten.
But could there be an inkling in this landscape,
These fields that wear the colours of abstention?
Here in County Monaghan, these drumlins
Took on, just yesterday, a chastened light,
A cold though oddly human character
Which chilled my spine and nudged me to remember
A moment from my ambling adolescence
When the balusters and clapboards on my street
Went dark, and trees that had companioned me

Through half my childhood suddenly looked strange.
As it happened, what had charged their leaves
With an eerie green and made the shadows black
Was nothing more uncanny or unwonted
Than an annular eclipse—my first and best,
Of which all others have been replicas,
Or parodies, or answering refrains.
But was there not an emblem in that moment,
Or should I say a lesson for the stumbler
I was and am—that inward-gawking pilgrim
Who in his first and second adolescence
Coloured the world with what he thought was passion
But was, in truth, a blotting of the sun,
In aspect marvelous, in substance normal,
Its beauties gorgeous but ephemeral?
Under the influence of that convergence
Of sun and moon, nothing was what it seemed,
And what it seemed was grossly simplified,
Its features doctored preternaturally.
How else explain the late October morning
When she and I were riding on a train
To Boston, both exhausted, both in need
Of something stronger than our morning coffee—
Something to clear our heads and clean our lenses
And show us to each other, warts and all.
I have the grace to blush when I remember
That at the time I'd dubbed her My Beloved,
Misnaming both desire and its object
And puffing in her face a kind of vapour
Through which she drew her breath as best she could.
And I was forty then—a little late
For making goddesses of common mortals
Or lowering a spiritual tiara
On anyone's unkempt, bewildered head.
Yet lower it I did, and more's the pity,
For while I turned my efforts to installing
Halo after halo on her brow
I must have missed a thousand other things—
The rocking railway car, the passing landscape,

The conversation in the seat behind us,
The negro porter gliding down the aisle.
I do remember, now, a dowager
Who thought that we'd eloped, and told us so,
And another, drooping low, exuding talcum,
Who inquired if the lady might be sick.
Other than those two, I can't remember
Anything at all of our environs,
So keen was I on tending to the needs
And savouring the grace of my beloved,
Who by this time had fallen fast asleep
Though not exquisitely, a glob of jam
Adhering firmly to her open mouth.
Cocked back against her headrest, looking less
The goddess than the victim of assault,
She stirred and snored—a noise, that had I heard it
For what it was, might well have been a klaxon
Warning of disasters yet to come.
And had I then the prescience to decipher
The message in her hard, downturning mouth,
The portent in the cracks beneath her makeup,
The cold self-hatreds hiding in her eyes,
I might have spared the two of us the anguish
Of savage separation—she departing
A few months later, wanting nothing more
Of my relentless, spotless adulation,
Which was at first her sustenance and joy,
A radiance exceeding her deserts,
But was at last a noisome silhouette,
A crazed intruder blocking out the light.

IV

A lot of snash and blathers, snapped the curate,
By which I mean the lout behind the bar
At the Black Bush—my temporary parish,
Where some of us had gathered to replenish
Our stores of knowledge and percipience,
Opining freely on the foolishness
Of Chamberlain, the excellence of Rommel,
And drifting over several pints of Guinness
To the Gaelic pastorale of de Valera—
The western paradise where handsome hurlers
And virgin maidens gambol in the sun.
The innocence of that Edenic vision
Elicited the curate's interjection
But woke in me a kindlier response,
Bringing to mind the image of my son
In bathing trunks, and prompting me to wonder
Yet again at my propensity
To train my purest, fiercest concentration,
My mind's engine and my heart's desire
On the one thing that can or will not stay.
How transient the hour when I stood,
Expectant, at the bottom of the slide
To watch him mount the ladder, step by step,
And at my urging, hurtle down the chute,
Fear and delight commingling in his eyes.
What was it but a second innocence
To watch his first adventures on the rug,
His shaky steps and partial comprehensions—
Or to hold him steady while he ventured out
Ten feet, then twenty, on his yellow bike
And having gained his balance, rode alone?
How transient the hour when I told him
The story of The Dragon Who Ate Stars,
While overhead the glowing constellations
Pasted to his ceiling faded out

And he himself devolved into his dream.
Of course it would have opened over time,
That gap between a father and his son.
But for the two of us those hours ended
Abruptly with Her Ladyship's departure
And what is called a legal separation,
Its violence undoing what was woven
With tact and patience, hour after hour.
I must have had a notion it was coming.
It must, in fact, have occupied my mind
Unconsciously the afternoon we wrestled
On the warm sand and played our favourite game,
A test of skill invented by myself
And aptly titled Knocking Daddy Over.
The rules were simple. I would sit crosslegged,
As if beneath the Bodhi tree, and he,
Taking a run of twenty feet or more,
Would fling his body's flying, flailing weight
On Daddy, who would gamely topple over,
Lifting him by his torso as he passed,
A tiny glider wafting into sand.
That afternoon I changed the rules a little,
Stopping his progress and the flow of time.
What was it but my effort to arrest
The present and to fortify the moment—
My choosing on an impulse to impede
His passage and immortalise his flight,
Holding him aloft against the sky
And framing, if I could, the moving face
That was, in small, a mirror of my own?
How lasting and how delible his laughter.
How transient that moment in the sun.

VI

Across the Water
Dublin, 1950

> *What is more fluid, more yielding than water?*
> *Yet back it comes again, wearing down the rigid*
> *strength that cannot yield to withstand it.*
>
>   Lao Tzu

III

Weigh your words. That terse imperative,
So laden with its own significance,
Has stayed behind, its author long since vanished.
What weight it carried in my childhood
I couldn't say, commingled as it was
With other cautionary admonitions.
Don't jump off the porch. You'll break your arches.
Check your facts. Don't forget to signal.
Now, when I think of it, it brings to mind
The image of the two of us at cribbage,
His pointer not a fatherly pronouncement
But a tender nudge, a mild *obiter dictum*,
Attendant to his playing of a Queen,
His pegging forward. *Fifteen-two, fifteen-*
Four, fifteen-six, and a pair is eight,
And a pair is ten. And a Sunday afternoon,
Moving at the tempo of our pegs
Around the bend, our quiet competition.
How could I be other than who I am,
Having as my mentor that exemplar
Of weights and measures, counting out his hand?
Read 'em and weep—or merely tally them
And in the future try a little harder.
Yet in the backwash of a windy Friday,
Replete with showers from the Irish Sea,

I thought of him again—and not in the way
That others saw him—not the Principal
Whose presence, unannounced, could silence children
And bring a sudden pallor to the classroom—
But as the architect and engineer
Who built a stage-set for electric trains,
A plaster landscape, mountainous and stark,
And at the centre cut an oval hole
Where he would sit, surveying everything.
Perhaps it's just the layering of the years
Or the vagaries of memory compounding
Amalgams out of disparate events:
Whatever it may be, that fluent force
Has caused me more than once to see my father,
Content within the circles of his trains,
As the emblem of the father he became
In twenty years, his stricken body shrunken,
His hair abruptly white, his plans cut short.
Ringed by relatives and smiling friends,
Who'd made a tacit pact to reassure him
And not divulge the truth of his condition,
He lay confused and charitably betrayed,
His knowledge circumscribed by good intentions.
His only son, it fell to me to sever
The ligaments of that benign deception
And penetrate the folds of his illusion.
Never before or since have I more gravely
Weighed my words or watched their slow descent,
Their import settling darkly as they fell,
As though it were a shadow before a storm
Or water spreading freely over stone.

IV

How well the bandsmen keep us from ourselves,
The black anxieties and desolations
And the cold dampness of a Dublin morning
Dissolving in a Sunrise Serenade.
How well the voices on the wireless,
So thick with portent and authority,
Invent a solid, auditory world
Where speech is the progenitor of action
And all those solemn makings and unmakings,
Those untried treaties and alliances,
Are not less tangible or permanent
Than cornerstones or plaques on public buildings.
The truth is otherwise, but in the light
That streams across my sofa in the morning,
A sentence spoken forty years ago
Can echo with the resonance of rosewood
And seem as recent as the latest news.
'You're not *my* son.' It came without a warning.
And I, the newly disinherited,
Sitting across from her, could hardly know
Whether to take her angry words to heart
Or let them go, so level was her tone.
It was, I trust, no act commensurate
With that remark which set it into motion.
A startled hare, it bolted from the bushes
And then was off—a disappearing fluff
Of white. Not so its psychic indentation,
Which shows no sign of wear or weathering,
Its colours changing slightly with the years,
Its shape intact. On Lower Baggot Street
I heard my inner voice repeating it
As though it were the remnant of a mantra
And I, the unbeliever, were for once
Believing in the power of the word
To outlast depredations and erosions
And speak its meanings even to the grave.
Yet what could be less solid than the voice

That spoke these words—a voice that in its prime
Rang out with epithets and imprecations
But at the end grew thin and timorous—
A weary walker, trudging in and out
Of what is often called reality,
Remembering her savings to the dollar
But jumbling cousins, uncles, aunts, and friends
And spelling even the smallest words aloud.
Holding her hand and listening for hours,
Her fellow patients bleating in their corners,
The air a stifling blend of disinfectants,
I seldom spoke—but was once more her son,
Our worst fears forgotten or denied,
Our differences resolving in a bond
Beyond our speech or conscious understanding.

V

Thy will be done, intones the congregation,
As if it were as effortless as breathing
To let that lust for absolute control,
For order in the chambers of the heart
And purpose in the churnings of the world,
Dispel itself in painless exhalations
And by an act of sufferance allow
Its crusts to be dispersed across the water.
Not that it can't happen in the still
And speechless centre of an ordered mind—
Nor that a mind as willful as my own
Must be forever pinioned to volition.
Rather that these shiftings to and fro,
These turnings and returnings of the will
Across its own habitual terrain,
Will be suspended only for a time
Before the beast that calls itself the mind
Gets up to fetch its meal and buy its paper
And render its unqualified opinion.
The water will hold you up, I told myself

And for the better portion of an hour
I let myself subscribe to that belief.
Taking my evening constitutional
Down Gilford Road and out along the Strand,
I entertained the notion that those waves
Travelling the width of the Atlantic
And entering the depths of Dublin Bay
Were present at my moment of conception
And had for fifty years transported me
From one discrete occasion to another.
It was at most a fleeting fantasy,
Disrupted by the screeching of the tram
And the sight of dirty children flinging sand.
But for the brief duration of that dream
I heard a semblance of my father's voice
Speaking a soft endearment to my mother
And saw that in the matter of my birth,
As in the framing of my destiny,
There was no law nor order nor control
But only instinct, chance and circumstance
Converging in an ever-changing pattern,
To which I still attach my signature
And lend the favour of an Irish blessing
But haven't the prerogative to alter
Or the temerity to call my own.

Dark Pool

(2004)

Sentence

i.m. Marion Howard (1905-1971)

Where are you now, if not within this hand
That moves as steadily across the page
As you in life processed within the span
Allotted you, your sentence and your song?

Dark Pool

I

Tomorrow something new may cross my path
But today I write to you from Dublin City,
Whose name, as you well know, is anything
But new. Along with torcs and other relics,
The Danes who lived and moved in these environs
Left behind an image and a name.
Whatever I may think when I look out
On Georgian squares beset by noisy traffic,
The Danish eyes that fastened on this landscape
Perceived in it a place of murky water,
To which they gave the Danish name for *dark*
And the Danish name for *pool*, which in the dark,
Unending stream of naming and re-naming
Became *dubh linn*, its Irish counterpart.
And so I write to you this Monday morning
From the Dark Pool, whose air is often damp,
As though its early name had lingered on,
Exuding into air no longer Danish
Or altogether Irish something wet
And dark—the residue of habitation
But also of the languages that came
And went, the words no weightier than ours
That now are part of that unseen deposit
Which lies on walls and lanes and kitchen gardens
And sometimes smothers what it claims to know.

II

Henry Street. Not recently or ever
Have I known any personage whose name
Became a street or avenue or lane,
Much less a thoroughfare or monument.
Some names are monstrous, others visible
Only under lens or microscope.

Whoever Henry was, his name attests
More to someone's estimate of value
Than to a lasting memory of Henry,
Who is not technically anonymous
But is, if I may venture such a judgment,
Functionally extinct. As for his name,
It has, I think, the status of a leaf,
Albeit one in tin, securely fastened
And seeming on a late-September day
As likely to survive him as those statues
Bearing the names *Parnell*, *Moore*, *O'Connell*.
Yet only yesterday, when I picked up
A history of the Easter insurrection,
I read that at the peak of their rebellion,
The joists and plaster of the G.P.O.
Crumbling on their dream of Irish freedom,
The poet-rebels tunneled from that building
And into Henry Street, there to establish
A last defense against ordained defeat,
A stay against inevitable surrender.
What do I know, I asked myself not once
But twice, so sweeping was my ignorance,
So deaf my ears to overtones of meaning,
Which in the Irish psyche resonate
As clearly as the Angelus at twilight,
Despite the bleats of cell-phones on the sidewalks,
The near-incessant roar of Dublin traffic.

III

Where are you now, that I should write to you
From this bewildered city? I call it that
To capture if I can its quick-step tempo,
Its harsh brasses and, no less than that,
Its rattling drums. I mean no disrespect
To the Dark Pool nor to its thousand years
Of history, its celebrated streets
Where authors in their cups and noisy poets

Maintained the gardens of their verbal Eden;
Where untold creatures clamoured to be named
And giants suited to that grand vocation
Threw out a dozen sumptuous appellations
For every beast that lumbered into view.
Dark Pool indeed! City of the Names,
I might have called it—names for enemies
And friends, cousins and acquaintances,
Passions and their objects, furtive feelings,
And all the dreck not spoken of in public
But named within the confines of the heart
And later brought to light. Bewilderment
Is not too strong a word for that emotion
Which sometimes overtakes me on these sidewalks,
Congested as they are with men and women
In earnest attitudes and in a hurry.
Such was the case one Friday afternoon
When everyone was headed to a bar
Or seemed to be, and I was out of step,
A foreigner with letters on his mind,
The ones I should have written earlier
To friends and family, retailing stories
Heard in the pubs or overheard in buses
Or clipped from pages of the *Irish Times*.
Those anecdotes more present in my mind
Than what was happening before my eyes,
I found myself accompanying the crowd
Into a pub whose name I can't remember,
Though I can see its stools and leather benches,
Its swirling smoke, its animated faces.
Maybe it was the Dublin intonation,
The *tink's* and *grands's* and *brilliant's* in the air,
The talk that was the sound track to the dramas
Occurring in the booths or at the tables—
Whatever it may have been, that dense profusion
Was like a storm, a bout of ugly weather
That I had wandered into, unprepared
And not well suited to negotiate.
Pausing at the counter, undecided

Whether to add more wind to that commotion
Or leave the way I came, as yet unnoticed,
I felt a word expanding in my mind
And pressing for release. The word was *publish*,
Untainted by its modern acceptation
And meaning, as of old, to interject
A private truth into the public body,
To make one's feelings known in public forum.
And as I entertained that potent word,
So rich in consequence and implication,
I found my tensions easing and my mind
Reflecting on the fabric I had entered,
Which someone aptly named a *public house*,
A shelter, if you like, for *publishers*,
However circumspect their revelations
Or cautious their impromptu publications.
Lifting my pint of Guinness, newly pulled
And primly handsome in its priestly collar,
I took my place among the publishers
And offered to the stranger on my right,
A nodding lad, inclined to conversation,
The essence of my thoughts on Irish weather.

IV

What is a name if not a bolt of fabric,
Its shape and aspect tailored and adorned
To suit the common good? One Friday morning
I lifted up mine eyes to the horizon
Whence came no help and only a little light,
The weather being damp and overcast,
The sky a dull and unrelenting grey.
Against that muted glow, revolving slowly,
A yellow crane attended to its business,
Some heavy object dangling from its cables.
What caught my eye and held my rapt attention
Was propped above the weights behind the cab,
Its presence no less bright for being small.

It was, I saw, the flag of the Republic,
Its triple colours flapping in the wind.
Imagining the man who climbed the ladder
And crawled out on the beam to mount it there
I felt a shuddering of vertigo,
As though it were myself who set that emblem
Of nationhood and long-sought independence
Aloft above a busy, fabled city
Which may or may not notice or regard it
Or find in orange, green, and neutral white
Its true identity. I looked away
And down, no native and no patriot
But stirred to wonder by a piece of cloth,
Whose form was changing even as I watched,
Its meaning not to be interpreted
But left to cast its net on crowded streets
And engines racing to the latest fire.

V

When does a common thing become a name
To be pronounced, intoned, interpreted,
Until the presence of the thing itself
Dissolves within the noise the noun is making?
That question crossed my mind as I was walking
In Stephen's Green on a Sunday afternoon,
Remembering the time I heard the word
Collective, liking its liquid consonants,
Its quiet vowels and its gentle burst
Of energy, as though a cloud had spoken.
Little did I know that in a word
So pleasing to the ear and to the tongue
There lived a history of violence,
A chronicle of griefs and deprivation,
Of manacles and chains and executions,
All in the name of some *collective* good
Which justified the evils it propounded.
What faith remains when names replace the things

Entrusted to their care? That afternoon,
The ducks in Stephen's Green were diving. Dipping
Into the water and out, in quest of tidbits,
They fit, or so I thought, their names: they *ducked*
And *ducked* again, their comic act restoring
An old congruity of word and thing,
As though the first to name those feathered shapes
Had got it right: had said what he had seen.

VI

Who shall be nameless, goes the politic
Expression, leaving us to conjure out
Of reference and tone the missing persons,
Who may be nameless to their dying days
But nonetheless appear as living shades
Acting and reacting on that stage
We set before our eyes. What matter, now,
If swarthy Jack was really Anthony
And winsome Jill was really Madeline?
I think of them this morning, Jack and Jill,
Who sat across from me, as nearly joined
As any could be on a public bus
Jouncing down a street in Sandymount
Oblivious of me, as of those others
Who read their paperbacks or sat in silence,
Jack and Jill were visibly enthralled
By what they had created, hand in hand
And lip on lip, its presence palpable.
I tried myself to be oblivious
But found my gaze returning to their faces,
So rapt were they in worship of their god.
That was twenty years ago or more.
And though those devotees have long since tumbled
Into a vale I'd rather not envision,
They stay in memory as in a vase,
Where dried stems may yet arrest attention
And dried blooms remain without a name.

VII

    They're waiting for a day or two, my friends
In Templeogue, to name their newborn daughter.
Will she be Lily? Deirdre? Margaretta?
They're saying nothing, letting us remain
Pleasantly in suspense, and letting her
Who presently is nameless have her day,
Unburdened by the garment she will wear
On every future day, the heavy ulster
Which may or may not suit her temperament,
But will, for life, be hers to don or carry.
So let me celebrate, this Sunday morning,
The blessed freedom of an unnamed child.
And let me recognise, as best I can,
That infant's counterpart, who may yet dwell
In every mortal frame that walks the planet
And every smattering of skin and bone
That lies beneath a name inscribed in granite.
To write a letter to that nameless one
Who in myself appears from time to time,
Unmarked by passion or adversity
And all the ills to which the flesh is prone—
To write a letter, asking her forgiveness
Or failing that, her tolerance and grace,
Could be the occupation of a lifetime,
A project suited to my later years,
A correspondence worthy of the effort.
For now, I lift my cup to that small soul,
So full of cries but empty of a name,
Who soon enough will have not one but three,
Each name a gate, a portico, a window.

VIII

    How loftily the pundits speculate
About a future no one will decipher
Even in retrospect, employing names

To do the work of knowing and unknowing,
The shaping and reshaping of the story.
What Jane will call a *splendid revolution*
Will seem to Joan a *spurious rebellion*
And facts themselves will gradually unravel
As sweaters do, their yarns at last returning
Into that primal state from whence they came.
Yet if I may join that happy band
Of prophets, panelists, and charlatans
Who claim to have a purchase on the future,
Allow me to envision Dublin City
In fifty years, its National Museum
Still the same, though newly stocked with cell phones
And other relics of our present time.
Its air will be more redolent of Progress,
Its Liffey even filthier than now,
Its urban essence all too effable.
As for the culture that sustained itself
On words and stout, as others have on wine,
What will become of it? My guess, as good
As anyone's, is that its bronze memorials,
Its Kavanagh and Anna Livia,
Its lanky Jimmy with his walking stick,
Will outlast all of us, a fitting tribute
To writers whom the world has deigned to honour.
But as for what those Publishers have published,
Those writers written in their finer hours,
I see it too as gradually disbanding,
As though the names that gathered on a page
Or in a room had gone their separate ways
And every text were headed for perdition.
Looking down this evening at the Liffey,
I see the waves dispersing on the quay,
The wakes dissolving in the fleeting light,
And wonder if those poems learnt by heart
Or cherished under glass in dustless rooms
Are any more coherent or substantial.
If not, then let the *dubh linn* claim its own,
The Names give up their portions to the stream.

And let it flow as mightily as water,
This language that is neither yours nor mine
But enters and inhabits us, its colours
As varied as the colours of the world,
Its lanes and crescents, channels and canals
As trafficked or as desolate as those
The eye encounters on its daily rounds
And shores against incipient erasure.

Leavings

Today I write from Meg's Uptown Café
On Castle Street, where someone's scarred guitar
Keeps company with someone's violin,
The two of them suspended from their pegs
On plaster that could use a coat of paint.
Who built those instruments and who performed
Sonatas and partitas, gigues and fugues,
Or, more likely, reels and Kerry slides,
Are matters for a morning's contemplation.
Even as I sip my bitter tea
And make the best of under-scrambled eggs,
I'm thinking of an air by Paganini,
In which the pure, impassioned violin
Ascends above the chords of the guitar
And occupies an atmosphere of longing
But in the end, as if to gratify
The need of all things light to live on earth,
Comes down in one reverberant cadenza.
It's raining now, as often in Tralee.
And as those anxious walkers on the pavement
Bow their heads to meet the brutal weather,
I'm hearing yet again that high cadenza
As though it were a trace in these environs,
A relic no more visible than want
Or memory, desire or speculation,
But nonetheless as present as the stench
Of cigarettes, those odours from the kitchen,
These bits of bacon cooling on my plate.

Holy Water

Was it a drink I wanted? Walking past
The public benches and the public toilets,
The roses in the garden, worse for wear
But still exuberant on trellises,
I turned into a churchyard, where the stones
Took on the slanted light of early evening
And voices softened, not in reverence
So much as confidence or privacy.
Strolling through the shade of the cathedral,
I found myself positioned by a wall
From which a faucet jutted, featureless
But for the metal sign above the spout.
Holy Water. Not a caption, really,
Nor yet a cataloguer's designation
But something more insidious than that,
A sort of invitation to a party
Or more respectfully, a gathering
To which I had no conscious inclination.
Speaking in Roman characters, it held me
Long enough to wonder where it came from,
That latent spirit cloistered in a pipe,
Its fluent cadence silenced by a valve
Though primed to be released at any moment.
All it would have taken was a turn,
A counter-clockwise motion of the hand.
What was it stopped me? Say it was a sense
Of something tangible behind my shoulder,
By which I mean no priest or risen ghost,
Much less a stern protector of the State,
But something I'd brought with me to Tralee,
A figment of a once and future longing.
Would that it might sustain me or be gone.
Would that I might pass and leave no trace.

Fidelities

What heart can know itself?
　　　ANTHONY HECHT

I

Coal dust thickens on my palate. Eight
o'clock: too early for the gardeners
and the workman with his scythe, who yesterday
cut wide swathes through weeds and knee-high grass.
Too early, too, for that conglomerate
of lies and vows, of true and false desires,
to fashion its imaginings from clay,
or wreak its mess, or work its synthesis.
Call it the heart. Or call it nothing more
than compost piled at the garden's edge,
contaminated silage. Now to look
inward is to watch an untilled field
lighten and darken like an overture
whose instruments have more than they can manage.
The score is treacherous. And each mistake
leaves that much more to ferret and unfold
from such small findings as avail themselves,
their secrets hidden in a turn of phrase
or trick of harmony, their fragile poise
lost and recovered as their form evolves.

II

This Irish dampness strews its melancholy
sweetness over the fields. Those cattle nosing
up to the fence, swishing the flies away,
could teach me, once and for all, how unavailing
and how ungracious appetite can be,
lumbering toward its apple-branch and choosing
nothing but what's before it. And every stray

desire, every random hankering
held back or satisfied, as it may happen.
Where will it end, that lust for foreign things—
or things made foreign by a change of light,
a shift of wind? Returning to the tonic,
the cadences confirm their origin,
call out their names. The coloratura sings
on key. And here, as if to clear its throat,
the northern sky grows brilliant, seraphic—
before relapsing to a common gray,
which in its steady dampness may appease
an appetite for permanence and vows
and in its bleakness pass for constancy.

III

Beneath these fluctuating waves, those currents
persist in changing light. The reeds hold still;
the evening contracts. To look beneath
this surface is to wait upon a friend
who will in time appear, his coat and pants
dripping, his eyes intelligent and tranquil.
What he will tell you of a changing earth
whose changes have no purpose and no end
will not suffice. Nor will his recitations,
thrown out above the water's ostinato,
do more than guide you to that other scene,
that nightly theatre of unformed thought,
where characters in livid conversations
remake their lives; where lovers come and go
in semblances and parodies of action,
and brutal acts advance a shapeless plot.
Call it your heart. Or call it your asylum,
its hours measured by a muffled gong,
its speech the bleatings of a foreign tongue
spoken in haste, under a foreign emblem.

Elegy
for Fred Hanna's Bookshop (now Eason-Hanna's)

The name remains but nothing of the floor-
to-ceiling shelves, the dusty intimacy.
Now the aisles are wide, the rubrics neat.
The checkout clerk waits by her computer.

Call it Progress. Call it What is Good
for Commerce. Not so good for you and me,
who came here to be neighboured by a culture
whose face was plain, whose heart was writ on paper.

Not that every author pleased our palates
nor that their world was kind, benevolent,
or just. Rather that it spoke to us,
its voice now hoarse, now sweet, but always human.

The Growing Poem

We cut it back, the lavish forsythia
whose branches had grown thick and interlocked,
their high arcs intertwined with untrained limbs,
blocking light and hampering the view.
How dwarfed it looks, its green insignia
returning week by week, its trunk-wood hacked
to knee-high stubs, from which resurgent stems
extend themselves, bearing a leaf or two.
I think of it this morning, reading lines
and cadences that will in time be chopped
to half their length or cut out altogether,
the opened space an aperture for light
and for such meanings as reside in zones
not clogged with word or matter. Managed, cropped,
and vulnerable to every sort of weather,
the growing poem seeks its perfect height,
as though its syllables were born of soil
and circumstance, its predicates of water,
its eloquence of rain and wintry air
replete with light and redolent of toil.

Perennials

Cut back, the gardens once again recede
to what they were before the wild buddleia
impaired our view, presenting to the eye
its own exuberant stems, its lilac mansions.
Cut down, the once-imperial cardinal flower
no longer calls attention to itself
nor do those gray, aggressive artemisia
occupy a ground that might have been
their own, so lasting was their residence,
so prevalent their spreading silver mounds.
Would that you and I, grown slightly older,
might find our counterparts in quinces pruned
and roots protected by decaying leaves.
Would that we might certify ourselves
as occupants of once and future gardens,
our worst proclivities deposited
beneath a hacked but still-resilient plant,
our memories encased in husks and cauls
or lifted like those dahlias, two by two,
and stored in sacks, as if there were no winter.

Currencies

The sky will write no signatures this morning
and post no bills. Something communicates
its loss in days as overcast as this,
the air so thick and damp as to diminish
commerce between free thought and these returning
leaves, this light that asks for nothing. Rates
change; the sidewalks crack; the happiness
recounted once too often turns to cash,
its graven face negotiable but torn
and mutilated by the dailiness
that falls between the moment and its ghost,
the night experienced and the night recalled.
Better to store the moment in its urn,
the cherished touch in silent consciousness,
the day in speechless praise. Or count the cost
in memories depleted or annulled
by alphabet and stanza. Here and now,
the lilacs have gone by; the purple phlox
reach from the ditch; and in its cloister *vox
humana* deigns to record or disavow.

The Swinging Door

I. Reticence

What is it but an envelope devised
to shelter those invisible desires,
those petty bigotries and rancid fears,
which would, if not protected, be exposed

for what they are? What is it but a bolt,
which keeps the stores of memory secure,
lest your house be looted by that burglar
who knows your slightest move, your subtlest habit,

your grossest fault? But what your barriers
have held at bay is not that predator
alone, nor yet the tireless voyeurs,

but that constrained intruder in your heart,
whose business is to see you as you are,
however much you keep yourself apart.

II. Release

What have you wanted more than that release
from isolation? Even a fleeting touch
on fingertip or wrist extends the reach
of your awareness to a foreign place

beyond this cell of silent contemplation,
so spacious in its way but so immune
to news of others' triumphs and misfortune.
Why then do you recoil in agitation

from inquiries and friendly overtures,
as though they might contaminate the pure
and noiseless air, the dustless atmospheres

in which, if you could have them, you would live,
your element a rectifying fire,
your silence no less potent than your love?

III. Shutters

In you, as in the closing of a chest
replete with cardigans and blocks of cedar
and lending to its ambience an odour
at once arcane and quietly robust,

I see the gestures of a temperament
responsive to itself as to the season,
as eager to be shut as to contain,
all summer long, each neatly folded garment.

Where will it end, that cycle of disclosure
and closing-up, advancement and retreat?
Within the moments of your timed exposure

I see a lens preparing to be shuttered,
as though the truest movement of your heart
were systole, your truest words unuttered.

IV. Interrogations

Is it for me that you have worn a mask,
its fixed mouth and inward-turning eye
suggesting caution or humility
or something in between? And when I ask

questions of the face that I encounter,
day by day and year by passing year,
is it a looking glass or two-way mirror
that you present to me, its hidden centre

there, or never there? Were you to answer,
I would consider what you had to say,
as though it held the truth of your desire,

wondering all the while if what I'd heard
were your confession or your kind reply,
your artful parry or your final word.

Forecast

for Alexander

    One day soon *Lobelia cardinalis*,
now a purple badge against the dried
cypress chips, a spreading fleur-de-lis,
will rise into the tallest of those plants
we chose last year, the brilliant cardinal flower.
And one day soon, whatever we began
the autumn afternoon when you were born
will reach a height I haven't yet imagined,
as you proceed to your majority
and that prodigious plant which sons and fathers
grow in clay or loam assumes a shape
and coloration yet to be conceived
by you or me. Call it maturity,
the shedding of the last protective foliage
and that unveiling. Call it what you will,
it's happening to us as well as you,
even as the workers in the garden
unload new soil and loose into the air
a high, unearthly, celebratory shower.

    July, 1997

Lincoln's Hands

Life Mask and Hands of Abraham Lincoln
Leonard Wells Volk (American, 1828–1895)

Cast in bronze and silent under glass,
    they keep their peace amidst
the landscapes, the chat of passers-by.
    The left lies flat, as on
a letter; the fingers of the right
    curl around a handle.
How delicate but how decisive
    these sculpted fingers look,
as if they held, in lasting balance,
    the mollifying touch
and, when warranted, the will to strike
    or sever. *I now wish*
to make the personal acknowledgement
    that you were right and I
was wrong. So he wrote to General
    Grant on July 13,
1863. As though they flowed
    within these metal veins,
his accurate phrases cross my mind,
    their courtly eloquence
and candour undiminished. Tell me
    if this is how we last,
our words no more erasable than bronze
    or faces carved in stone.

A Given Name

for Joanne and Gary Mensinger

    i

Maquoketa. I think I heard it first
out of my father's mouth. A quiet town
in Iowa, it left me unimpressed
but for its name, which like a pleasing tune
heard on the radio, installed itself,
its savour growing stronger through the years.
Speaking *Maquoketa* now, I find myself
removed to where I lopped on wooden stairs
and fed fresh raisins to a cocker spaniel,
my mother vacuuming, my sister building
dolls from hollyhocks. Each syllable
could be a raisin, too, and each unfolding
consonant a sweetness on the tongue,
the name itself an elegiac song.

    ii

Des Moines. Clinton. Davenport. Dubuque.
As easily as breathing, I intone
those lasting names, as though no loss or heartbreak
had ever happened. Closed and long since gone,
Van Allen's grand department store in Clinton
has left its Louis Sullivan facade,
a convoluted signature in stone.
Part-Celtic, part-Corinthian, its dated
elegance recalls a finer time,
when cities spoke from throbbing civic hearts.
Today the shoppers, stocking home and farm,
avail themselves of bargains at the K-Marts,
forsaking Penney's and Montgomery Wards.
What stays are names and opulent facades.

iii

I hear them in the morning and the evening,
as though they signified familiar rooms
in musty public buildings: *Bath*, *Corning*,
Binghamton, *Elmira*. Foreign names
at first, they've lost their colours. Twenty years
of hearing them have made their flavours dull,
their structures no more striking than the spires
of friendly churches, charitable and local.
But will there come a time when I endow
those common places with the same affection
as now I sometimes feel when *Iowa*
comes up in revery or conversation
or makes its way, as patiently as bees,
into the papers or the evening news?

iv

I can't call back the years nor legislate,
by any act of naming, my return
to that remembered, half-imagined state
when name and home and family were one.
Nor can I make of *Iowa* a shelter
impervious to fashion or assault,
nor build of empty properties an altar,
nor carve from words a temporal retreat.
And yet I do just that, in speech and thought,
as though the names *Maquoketa* and *Clinton*,
uttered in reverence, could muster out
the tutelary spirit of a town
and by the glory of a given name
bestow the passing credence of a dream.

Greta

All day she lies
beneath the pin oak, leashed
to a post, her space defined,
her world encompassed by a nylon cord.

Looking away from us, she sees
those spruce trees in their mid-September colours,
the lilies still in bloom,
and, from time to time,
the neighbour's yellow cat, who keeps

his distance, stepping lightly.
What passes through her mind,
we wonder, watching her sphinx-like calm,
her easy vigilance.

And what, if anything, can we,
her keepers, know of that awareness,
which senses each incursion
and sniffs each unfamiliar,
uninvited odour?

And when she greets us, tail
swishing, tongue expectant,
does she not see a portion of ourselves
which we ourselves will never see,

though we outlive her lapping tongue,
her black, recumbent body?

A Winter Fire

i

Just yesterday, as if to inform myself
with news I'd made an effort to forget,
I listened to some chewings in my roof,
some feet across the rafters. What I'd thought
immutable—or built to last the decade—
was showing its unstable character
and scattering its dust above my head.
It might have been a lawsuit or a fire
or merely a new inflection in a voice
protesting permanence. Into the day's
apparent peace it sent its hungry mice
to eat my joists and short my circuitries.
Under the ribs of my apparent calm
it stirred the torments of another time.

ii

What matters in these early morning hours
is not those fears and animosities,
those rankling slights and unrelenting worries
which block my light and taint my diaries
but what arrives half-noticed, half-expected:
a chill in the air, a sudden darkening
across the sill, a wrinkle in my forehead.
Were I to read those signs as souls returning
from some remote dominion of the dead
or find in them an emblem for those hurts
which are, for good or ill, our daily bread,
I'd miss the point entirely. Out of the night's
emptiness come inklings of a morning
devoid of thought and innocent of meaning.

iii

Insolent, unseemly, avaricious,
those intimations of a new disorder
in mind or body, flesh or consciousness,
intrude upon the pleasures of the hour
and the languor of a Sunday afternoon.
Talking unguardedly and sipping wine
on a friend's deck, I felt a sudden pain
beneath my belt, as though a tree had fallen
over a power line. Then less and less,
and the throbbing stopped. The conversation spread
its coat of meanings over that awareness
of something gone awry. Whatever dread
it wakened in my bowels and my brain
dissolved in words, its origin unknown.

iv

Merely to call them by their rightful names
is to see them as they are: *anxiety*,
unrest, *unease*. No longer will the pseudonyms
suffice. Contentment is not serenity,
nor anger rage, nor perturbation torment.
Awake at four, I heard the rise and fall
of my own breath and felt a hot resentment,
a tightened jaw, a pulsing in my temple.
What were the names for those indignities
which burned below the grate of conscious thought?
I called them *insults*, *lies*, and *travesties*
and drifted back to sleep. But what I brought
out of the heat of that nocturnal fire
came back to warm me in a winter hour.

Winter Night

The full moon emerges
through thinning cirrus clouds.
Over the spruce's top
it hangs, remote, unharmed.

My feet and hands are cold.
On the packed snow my soles
make squeaks but leave no tracks.
I know I am alive.

Come and See

Accompanied by hosta and impatiens,
Shakyamuni sits beneath the tree,
Famously serene and not at all
Concerned with what a doctrineless observer
Is thinking as he looks out on his lawn,

Making of spruce and pine and wild lupine
A composition he might call his own,
Were not its parts available to all,
Its order neither human nor inhuman
Nor wholly arbitrary. *Come and see,*

The Buddha is reported to have said,
Encouraging the blasting of conceptions,
A waking to the blackbird on the lawn
Who just now flew, too quick for any mind
To organize or order into stone.

Prose Should Be Transparent

Prose should be transparent, Orwell said,
A windowpane through which that cardinal
Rooting in the leaves for fallen seeds

Can be himself and not an English phrase
Exchanged for yet another over coffee
Or formed of ink, each character a flag

Run up a pole or draped below a window
To honour that incomparable bird
Who even now has flown, unharmed, unhindered.

A Discipline

Hardest of all, this month of February,
This isthmus with its snow and icy roads,
Its dripping eaves and dirty melting mounds.
How difficult to live in such a venue,
Which seems, on darker mornings, like a threshold
Before a door that will or will not open.

How urgent, then, to learn the discipline
Of living here in ugly February,
Not wanting days to end or calendars
To turn, but saying, *There you are, my friend*,
And *Here I am* to frozen creeks and rivers,
Which any day may melt and throw up floods.

Habits

How arrogantly they carry us
    into the pharmacy, the market,
        the bank, even the darkened bedroom,

as though we were the wafers on
    their tray, the pot of steaming tea,
        the empty cups. And we accede

most days, so innocent are we
    of their insidious intent,
        their will to make us inmates of

ourselves, incarcerate our longings,
    reduce our acts to replicas,
        our words to parodies, our smiles

to imitations. What happiness
    to send those sponsors on their way:
        to taste, at last, the tangerine,

the bowl of cereal set before us,
    the berries' ripe intelligence,
        the cup of coffee not yet cold.

Necessities

Merely to watch those juncos at the feeder,
Their language not the consonants and vowels
Of human speech but potent all the same,
Each flutter of the wings a dare or warning,

Suffices to recall him to the moment,
That watcher at the window who divides
The Better from the Best, the Not So Good
From what his shifting mind elects to value,

Forgetting that in this the present moment
Those gray-and-white arrivals at the feeder
Are taking what they need and nothing extra,
Each dip and turn a necessary gesture.

Westward

Why do poets in their advancing years,
When love of the word survives, but only barely,
Cleave to the long and fluid, half-prosaic line
As though it were a cable for rappelling
And not a tightrope any longer? Why do they write
As though the informing spirit had no checks
Or exigencies, no chastening vessel?
This afternoon in Prescott, Arizona,
Liz is making her travel plans, and I
Relax in the pickup, reading Carruth's long lines
That have the fluency of one who no longer cares
For the world's praise and the self's advancement,
Moving as freely as those cirrus clouds
In the Arizona sky. In truth,
I am neither old nor given to self-defeat,
But the freedom of those who no longer write for praise
Appeals to me, and the easy flow
Of Hayden's lines is a likeable illusion.
I think when I am old, when lines
Come slowly or not at all,
I will recall this piece of make-believe,
These lines so much at liberty with themselves,
This clear, unhindered western sky.

Heartwood

Is it not a second innocence,
this state of being fifty-nine,
just shy of that formidable
age of stature and attainment
if also of forgetting? Let

the chips fall, the shavings make
their mess beneath that steady blade
whose cut is deepening, whose teeth
approach a still, resistant core,
a place of origins and endings.

The Holy Alls
The Burren, 1950

I

   How did it happen that an Iowan
Without credentials or portfolio
Re-domiciled himself in County Clare
And having left his native ground behind him
Became its ill-prepared ambassador?
I've asked myself that question more than once,
Being myself that odd American
Or as I'm sometimes called in these environs,
The Yank who lives alone in Ballyvaughan
And sometimes can be found at Connor's pub
Sipping his whiskies with the best of them—
Or, more often, walking in the Burren,
Looking the part of someone's long-lost son.
How I might, on any given morning,
Construe the waking body I inhabit
Or greet the gander in my shaving-mirror
Or name his features, is another matter.
Stopping at the victualler's to chat
Or pausing in the market to inquire
After the health of someone's relative,
I sometimes cast myself as resident
Or fancy my identity as altered
Or, best of all, forget myself entirely,
Becoming yet another paper vessel
Floating in a common, human stream.
From that delectable hallucination,
Which bears the lure and danger of a dream,
I'm soon enough awakened: *You're the Yank
From Idaho. Whatd'ya hear from home?
Ya know, I have a cousin in Chicago . . .*
By all such enquires and salutations,
Heard recurrently in Connor's pub
Amidst the pipe-smoke and the smell of Guinness,

Am I protected from my own delusions,
Though in the end not wholly satisfied.
Conceived by staunch Midwestern Methodists
And reared a Christian in a river town,
Companioned as a child by fields of corn
And menaced by a temperamental river,
Am I forever to be understood
As but the minted product of those forces,
Its features formal and indelible,
Its image fixed, as on a wooden nickel?
That I should venture to define myself
Against the waters of Liscannor Bay
Or see the image of my aspirations
In congeries of megalithic stone
Is no less plausible, it seems to me,
Than seeing in a Methodist retreat—
A basement dinner, long on casseroles
But short on zest and sensuality—
A fitting emblem of my inmost nature.
In truth, the listing ship on which I've sailed
For fifty years has kept itself afloat
By twists and turns too numerous to mention.
And of the several flags I've travelled under
The one most suited to my heart's unrest,
As to my temperament, is neither blue nor red
Nor green nor orange but a neutral white.
At home, if I can call it that, the wide
Waters of the river pass the bench
From which I watched the towboats pushing barges,
Aware, as best I could be, that the passing
Of coal and steel was not unlike the stream
Which would in time transport my aging frame
From Eastern Iowa to County Clare,
The waters here more turbulent by half
But not invaded by commercial vessels
Nor shadowed by a Methodist's compunctions.

II

No silence ever came more suddenly
Than what I happened on in mid-July,
Having bestirred myself to take a walk
Across the most intransigent of landscapes,
A coastal stretch comprised of creviced rock.
A *boulder-meadow*, someone might have called it,
Were not its contours quite the opposite
Of anything hospitable or kind
To lost sheep or ramblers like myself.
Conjure, if you will, a sandless desert
In tones of gray, its western edge converging
With bands of shifting, pewter cumuli,
Its eastern border reaching out to sea.
Within the cavities between the rocks
The colonies of violet lobelia
Sent up their quiet message of survival,
As if to contradict a larger voice
Which spoke of poverty and stark extinction.
What am I doing here? I asked myself,
Feeling the bumps of stone beneath my feet
And picturing myself, if only briefly,
As a Methodist's impression of a pilgrim,
A thick-heeled parody of penitence
In search of something not unlike atonement.
I might have made a tale of that vignette,
A fantasy replete with pieties,
My infant spirit nursed on paps of stone
And succoured by the silence of the place—
A silence even I, a connoisseur
Of quietude and dank monastic places,
Had never quite experienced before.
As it happened, that unbroken silence,
So rich in resonance if poor in speech,
So redolent of absence and abstention,
Was soon to be dismantled by the advent
Of startling company. At first a scarfed
Silhouette, a set of toiling shoulders.

Moving across a monochrome of stone,
Her presence soon took on its full proportions.
"A cold day," she said, as if the shawl
Wrapped securely round her coiled arms
Weren't evidence enough. Across its folds
Her black hair fell in runnels, flecked with gray.
"It is indeed," I said, and from that small
Aperture there flowed the usual
Banalities and customary phrases,
A stream of speech that widened as we walked,
Bearing in its waters bits of old
Biographies, the sticks if not the stones,
The stories that accompany a self
Over the boundaries of state and nation
And stay afloat through winding ways and decades.
From her I heard the story of a husband
Returned from war, his mind an aching muscle,
His heart a ghost. "A canister for drink,"
His well-wrought body swelled into a carcass
With which she lived, bruised but not disloyal,
But which at last she left, finding the stony
Soil of County Clare, where she was born,
A refuge from the dirty streets of Boston.
From me she heard the story of a wife
Gone off the rails—a noisy locomotive
Careening down a pebble-strewn embankment
And taking as its train the rumbling freight
Which her uncommon lust for acquisition
Had packed and lengthened, year by struggling year,
Its clanking boxcars bordered at the front
By her, and at the trailing end, by me.
"You were the red caboose?" my present consort
Made bold to ask. "I was indeed," I said,
"Though at the start I'd thought I was the tender."
Out of such assertions and exchanges,
Coloured, to be sure, by overtones
Of self-conceit and self-exoneration,

We fashioned something wider than ourselves
And less distinct—a fluid atmosphere
Within whose ambience those well-defined
Conglomerations called identities
Mingled in a shapeless, shifting wash
Which neither she nor I could call our own.
Over the course of many stony miles,
Accompanied by gulls and crashing surf,
We clambered over knee-high fieldstone walls
And helped each other over crevices,
Talking all the while. But only hours
Later, when the temperatures was falling,
Did we compare our first, erroneous
Impressions. "You know," said she, "when I first heard
Your voice, I could have sworn that you were Irish."
And that, she added, was the honest truth,
Or as they say, "the holy alls of it."
I, in turn, confessed that in her speech
I'd heard the tones of an American,
Retuned, or so I'd thought, by County Clare
And tempered by the wear of Irish weather.
Was it the joint force of those disclosures
That parted us—or merely the signs of rain?
I couldn't say. But in their aftermath,
We went our ways, promising to meet
Again on some fortuitous occasion,
As though by meeting we had made the sign
Of infinity or cut a figure-eight
On water no more stable than ourselves,
On ice no less resurgent than our lives.

V

    Hear it as undulant courante,
Whose formal pattern changes by the second,
Revealing to the world and to oneself
The vagaries and checks, the graceful turns
And not-so-graceful lurchings of the spirit,

Which, had it never ventured such a caper,
Had never known itself. To that bold dance,
Which once was called the making of a soul
And now is called the finding of a self,
I pay the homage of an ardent mind.
Am I no more than that imagined man
Whom I've invented, not to spare myself
The old constraints of county, state, and country
But merely to be free of those compulsions
Which come with being what you've always been
Or think you've been—a being twice defined
By place and parentage, its image stamped
And dated? *There you go*, that coin declares
To all who have an interest in the matter.
But am I not entitled to envision
A being neither struck nor carved on stone
By accidents of lineage, place, and nation?
Hear it as the pulse of generation,
That stirring at the centre of the heart,
Where sometimes in the evenings I repair,
As eager for the heart's arcane reportage
As for the suet of the evening news.
Warming my damp feet before the fire,
I sometimes suffer glimpses of a self
Beholden not to eastern Iowa
Nor to the foreign stones of County Clare
Nor even to its own unbounded nature
But wandering from spring to plain to delta,
Itself a wave in swift, unending water.
And sometimes in my reveries I'm joined
By my astute companion from the Burren,
Whose name, if I may speak it now, is Maire.
Hearing, as I often do, her stories
Of Irish hardships, dreams, and peccadilloes,
I sometimes travel freely to those places
Of which she speaks, becoming now a farmer
And now a priest, and now an Irish lover.
From time to time, our conversation turns
To that impenetrable conundrum

Of who we are, or were, or might become
Were circumstance consistent with desire.
And when she asks me, as she sometimes does,
To tell her in a nutshell what I *want*,
Or what, if I could have it, I would *have*,
I find myself adopting in my speech,
As in my turn of thought, her own inflections.
The holy alls of it, I want to say,
Referring to a self I've yet to see
But have, on certain nights, intuited—
A self without the usual partitions
Dividing it from leaf and lake and stone,
As from its neighbouring inhabitants
And any colour other than its own.
To think of such a self, as thin as silk
And no less porous, is to entertain
A solemn mystery, though not the kind
Accompanied by thurible or cantor
Or pondered mightily from lofty pulpits.
I see it rather as a stormy day
Without the storm, the treetops undulant,
The hillsides ready for a blast of rain.
And when I think of it, it's not a sacred
Text that comes to mind, nor yet a vision
Of angels loitering around an altar
But something altogether natural—
A sky where clouds are forming and unforming
Even as they pass. And add to that
The kestrel's flight, its attitude as clear
And purposeful as any sculpted form,
Its veerings no less strange for being familiar,
Its cry no less remote for being known.

Leaf, Sunlight, Asphalt
(2009)

The Glad Creators

Watching the light die along the canal,
Recalling the glad creators, all
Who'd played a part in the miracle . . .

    BRENDAN KENNELLY, *"Light Dying"*

i.m. May O'Flaherty

I

Had I been born a decade earlier
I might have found myself in Dublin City,
An able novice gamely setting out,
Equipped with confidence and cautious diction
But all the same a lamb among those lions
Who frequented McDaid's and Davy Byrne's,
Reciting Yeats or Ferriter by heart
Or bellowing invectives to the rafters
Or sitting meekly with a ball of malt.
I might have hung my hat with Kavanagh's
Or backed a horse that no one else believed in—
The counterpart, if I may say it plainly,
Of all those cherished scripts and precious verses
That never saw the light, or if they did,
Were not to be regarded or remembered.
I might have strolled along the Grand Canal
Or greeted Behan on an evening walk
Up Baggot Street, or stopped at Parsons Bookshop
To turn the pages of O'Connor's latest
Or, if lucky, met the man himself,
Smartly dressed and ripe for conversation.
What better place for scintillating talk
Than Baggot Street, its sun-reflecting fanlights
Looking down on realists and dreamers?
What better place than Dublin, all its glory
Tarnished just enough to make it human
And all its grace reduced but not abandoned.

II

"What *is* this?" asks the Zen contemplative,
Divining that the undistinguished street
He's seen a thousand times is not banal
But like Traherne's an oriental marvel.
"What *was* that?" I might ask of Dublin City,
Where words were not imperial adornments
Nor yet the currency of politicians
But were, it seems, the very nutriments
On which a culture aching for release
Fed its heart and fortified its mind.
"May your son become a bishop," Behan said
To the kind nun attending at his deathbed.
Outrageous, yes, but in its way humane.
What finer way to offer gratitude
Or fend off fear, than by the spoken word,
Flavored to be sure by irony
But none the worse for that. And afterward,
The solemn pageantry of hearse and drum,
Wherein the State that had imprisoned him
And banned his books saluted his cortege.
And all for doing nothing much of note
But writing well and speaking from the heart.

III

Rudest of men, Kavanagh compared
A foolish woman's animated mouth
To a skipping rope suspended from her ears,
As though conspicuous loquacity
Were neither to be savored nor admired
But treated as a breach of civic order.
Were that the case, Kavanagh himself
Might well have landed in a lightless cell
And spent his years conversing with the walls
Or venting his opinions to the vermin
Until, at last, descending into silence.
As it was, he spent his unencumbered,
Spacious hours in the Palace Bar

Conversing with the likes of Myles and Cronin,
As if to talk were not an irksome chore
But were, in truth, the stuff of life itself
And all the freight of adjective and adverb
Were not mere ornament or armament
But were the glowing essence of the world
Embodied in the freely spoken word.
How fitting that the bard of Baggot Street,
So long on notions and so short on tact,
Should find his truest locus in the sonnet,
That prison-cell of nuns and plaintive lovers,
And there compose his late insouciant songs
With only water to restore his soul
And only syllables for company.

IV

Flann O'Brien. Myles na gCopaleen.
A quiet man who rarely said a word,
He stored the richest treasures of his mind
Behind the masks of multiple personae.
Better to be silent than to cast
The one pearl before a crowd of mockers.
Better to retain it for the page,
Where, if all conditions were propitious,
Its lustre might endure. Who else but Myles
Would think to conjure out of Irish air
A ready cadre of ventriloquists
To escort dullards to the theatre,
Providing, thus, engaging repartee
For those less able than themselves? In time,
That cunning band, impatient with their pay,
Would stoop to threatening their witless charges.
"Deposit, sir, a fiver in my pocket
Or I will take the liberty of making
Salacious comments to your brother's wife."
Faced with such extortion, Dublin's dullest
Fell to writing notes to one another,
Lest some coarse inflammatory insult
Or subtle barb be channeled through their mouths.

In this, if in no other ways, they shared
The modus of their reticent creator,
Who played, at once, ventriloquist and dummy,
Maintaining silence when it served his need
Or speaking through his many-colored masks
Or giving voice to voices not his own.

V

Scourge of puritans and pietists,
He saw the self-invented Irish nation
As nothing nobler than a load of hay
Beneath whose weight the likes of Myles and Behan
Breathed as best they could. And yet he stayed,
His name no longer *Whelan* but *O'Faolain*,
And fashioned from his nation's wounded psyche,
As from its failing dreams, his master story.
O'Connell's flaws and De Valera's failures
And all the contradictions he recorded
Were, it seemed, refractions of his own.
A writer should be cold, he told O'Connor,
And ever-distant from his characters.
Yet what, if any, distance lay between
The seasoned author and his character,
A rough-hewn Mayo priest who found himself
Prevailed upon to bury an apostate?
The rogue had sent away his wife and children,
And lived for half a decade with his mistress,
Who now would have him buried as a Christian.
"I'll put a stop to that!" the priest declared,
But in the end, he nodded and consented,
Doing, we are told, "the human thing."
Could that not be a motto for O'Faolain,
Who was himself no stranger to temptation?
And what, in truth, inclined him toward the lady
Whose culture was as alien as England's
And whom he thought not beautiful but *stately*?
What but her words, as when she wrote of Dublin,
The most implacable buildings were lanced with light,

Or saw on Herbert Place a *sun-charged gauze*.
But was it words or what they signified
That caused a realist to choose romance
And wakened fancies in a skeptic's heart?

VI

Imagine, if you will, the well-stocked shelves
Of Parsons Bookshop and the well-worn stool
Where Kavanagh, who rarely cracked a book,
Studied racing forms or read his paper
Or flirted with the girl behind the counter.
Imagine him in tweeds, avoiding Behan,
Or turning to exchange a salutation
With Clarke or Montague or Mervyn Wall.
And if you're of a mind to offer blessings,
Then fashion one for May O'Flaherty
Who made a temple of a common shop,
A place of worship where the greenest poet
And hoariest of novelists could meet
And there pay tribute to that World of Letters
Which now we must envision through the lens
Of non-reflective glass, as if those pages
Typed on Remingtons and Olivettis
Were not the spirit's living monuments
But merely relics of another time.
And as for Miss O'Flaherty,
Imagine her discussing acquisitions
With Mary King, or freshening her window.
Or see her, now, in Owen Walsh's portrait,
A gray-haired, sensible, upstanding woman,
For whom the miracle of Parsons Bookshop
Was not the issue of a grand design
Nor yet the fruit of visionary thought.
"It was all an accident," she later said.
Had I been born a decade earlier,
I might have written sonnets in her honor
Or failing that, sung praises to her name.

Dublin in July

> *When the self advances toward the ten thousand things,*
>   *that is called delusion;*
> *When the ten thousand things advance toward the self,*
>   *that is called enlightenment.*
>
>   Eihei Dogen, *Genjokoan*

I

The Four Courts bear the heat of late July
And down Dame Street the buses wheeze and belch
Their foul exhalations, wearing ads
For *Women on the Verge of HRT*
And images of lissome men and women
Vacationing in Portugal and Spain.
Whatever I was thinking when that siren
Erupted from the din, its two notes blaring,
Was gone before I knew it, leaving only
A quick impression of a speeding engine,
A red-faced driver screaming out his window,
The heads and shoulders of pedestrians
Turning to watch the swiftly passing show.
Where is the stillness at the heart of things?
Where the silence? Here in the midst of movement
My own unquiet mind pursuing Dogen's
Notion that the hungry, angry self
Advancing toward the world creates delusion,
I listen for that stillness and that silence,
As though they might be heard in horns and sirens.

II

Take a walk down South Great George's Street,
Where seedy bars and not-so-great hotels
Consort with trendy restaurants and shops
And India commingles with Japan.

Here is a laundry, there an Oxfam outlet.
And everywhere the crowds, the jostling shoulders,
The cell phone bleating from a stylish belt.
Tonight we'll dine at Yamamori Noodles,
Tomorrow eat panini at the Bailey
Or Chicken Tikka at the Shalimar.
What has become of that revered, imagined
Dublin of O'Brien and O'Faolain,
Its taste as Irish as a ball of malt?
Look for it in Liverpool or Boston
Or conjure it yourself from pints of Guinness.
But here beware of Vespas when you cross
This street that's no more Irish than its name,
Where traffic comes in rolling, tidal swells
But now and then grows still, as if recalling
The ochre ethos of a slower time.

III

On Grafton Street the blonde contortionist
Taunts a man who leers, or seems to leer:
"We know what you're doing. Take your hand
Out of your pocket!" Flashing a practiced grin,
She bends her undulate, half-naked torso
Until her eyes are looking up her backside,
Her grin intact, her frame a human hairpin.
All that by way of warming up her body
And warming, too, the watchers who surround her
In attitudes of wonder and desire.
And now the main event, the fitting climax.
For no more money than would fill a hat,
She steps into a small, transparent cube
And rolls her supple limbs into a ball.
As though she were a relic under glass,
A sacred text preserved for contemplation,
She waits in stillness for the crowd's applause.
Call it if you must a holy show,
A spectacle unworthy of regard.
But did she not arrest the human tide
That now goes out, not waiting for her bow?

IV

The self advances to its hiding place,
This table where unnumbered pints of Guinness
Have left their autographs in broken crescents.
Revenants of raconteurs and poets—
O'Brien, Behan, Cronin, Kavanagh—
Come back to haunt this visitor, whose thirst
Is not so much for witty conversation
As for a stillness strangely to be found
Amidst the clinks of glasses and the slow,
Sustained consumption of a ball of malt.
High windows lend an air of the cathedral
And shed a friendly though impartial light
On malice and benevolence alike,
As though the bygone boos and panegyrics,
The lurid gossip and the florid tales
Of reputations won and quickly lost,
Were so much dust, now settled in its corner,
However bright its colors at the time,
However real its presence in this room.

Beyond My Ken
The Samsara Bar and Café, Dublin, 2004

The lights are low, the table lantern-lit.
How restful to be sitting in this place,
its bamboo screens suggestive of repose,
its sparse calligraphy replete with meanings
well beyond my ken. How fortunate
to find myself enclosed by these environs,
whose name means suffering, the never-ending
cycle of birth and death, the end result
of ignorance, aversion, and desire.
The waitress takes my order, unaware
that earlier tonight, unheralded,
a slender book was eased into the world.
I hold it to the lantern, knowing it mine,
but knowing also that its ink and paper
are no more mine than that calligraphy,
those rich, exotic dishes on the menu.
How apt to celebrate that glad event,
so long awaited and so much desired,
in this the palace of impermanence,
its charms a warning that no book will last
for very long, and therefore, should be relished,
as presently I'm relishing this plate
of steaming vegetables and fragrant rice
whose name I duly note but won't remember.

A Wish for My Sixties
for Michael Longley

I would have this setting down of words
Occur as naturally and, yes,
As fluently as sitting down
For conversation over fish and chips
And water in a paneled snug,
Our subjects—poetry, of course,
But also parenthood, Stravinsky—
No more important than the ease
Of two old poets having lunch,
Their words well-chosen, to be sure,
But also quick and unimpeded.

We Must Labor to be Beautiful

*True ease in writing comes
From art, not chance.* So spake
The arch-apologist
For craft that even craftsmen
May fail to hear or notice

If what is written sings
As easily as Anna
Moffo in her heyday
Or Mozart in his *Ave*:
Song that's made of rests,

Quarter notes, fermatas,
Chromatics, decrescendos,
But seems as effortless
As blood in healthy veins
Or water over stone.

Ease of singing comes
From scales, arpeggios,
The hour spent perfecting
A single trill or slur
Or glorious cadenza.

Why then should labor be
Demoted, disregarded,
Consigned to steerage while
The dancers flirt and twirl,
The dandies stroll and swagger?

And why should I, on hearing
Yet another lilting
Connemara air,
Mistake its craft for passion,
Its art for artless longing?

Leaving Tralee

What better place to set down furtive thoughts
than here at the Imperial Hotel
on Denny Street at seven in the morning?
Not so much imperial as mellow
and darkened by Victorian décor,
this dining room is vacant but for us,
that harried-looking waiter and the one
he waits on, namely me. As for the page
I'm writing over tea too hot to swallow
I see it as a sieve, through which the pungent
odor of last night's fish, the kitchen clatter,
the muted talk of patrons in the lobby,
and all the sights I have or haven't noticed
are passing to their final destination.
But even as I mutter my lament
for all things unredeemed, unrecognized,
I'm thinking of the Sunday afternoon
I pulled a yellowed journal from the shelf
and found in it the features of a dream
of which I had no other recollection,
no tension in the limbs or in the heart.
If it survives, that story of a ride
through cobbled streets in someone else's car,
it's in those sentences, themselves imperiled.
Lift up your voices, cries the aging hymn.
Lift up your cameras, your pens and notebooks,
lest the images that flash and fade—
those taut inflections in a fleeting voice—
be no more lasting than a passing thought
and no less formless than a jotted dream.

Original Face

*What was your original face
before your parents were born?*

    Zen koan

When you ask me to remember
my fundamental face,
my face before my parents
and ancestors were born,

I recall a photograph
of Marion and Beth,
who later would become
my father and my mother

but then were in their twenties,
courting or newly married
and gliding in a rowboat
on the Mississippi River.

Marion holds the oars
poised above the water.
Dashing in his cap,
he glances over his shoulder,

while Beth, a camera
cradled in her lap,
smiles, as if content
to be riding in a boat

with Marion, who leans
forward, about to make
another skillful stroke.
His shirt is loose and white,

her jacket square and dark.
Their indistinct reflections
ripple on the waters
of what appears to be

a quiet, easeful slough.
Beyond them, rows of trees
bend toward the right,
as if to counterbalance

their boat's gentle momentum.
What currents, even then,
were trafficking between them?
What thoughts of work or children?

Ahead of them lay hardship
and all the hoarded thought
of forty years together.
But here, as if misfortune

were but a passing phantom,
the two of them look ready
and eager for a future
that will, in time, include

the son who can't be seen
but nonetheless abides
somewhere in those waters,
those high Midwestern clouds.

Prune Kringle

Prune kringle, it was called.
My job: to bring it home
intact, its flaky crust

still warm, its dark interior
sweet, thick, delicious.
I was a boy of ten,

old enough to stand
in Allen's Tea Room, coins
in hand, to count my change,

and safely to transport
that soft, mysterious treat
swaddled in cellophane.

Old enough, as well,
to feel your gratitude,
your pride in my attainments,

but not yet old enough
to know what care or pains
you took in my behalf

or what your worries cost
in sleep or muffled tears.
I was a thankless child,

and yet my weekly errand,
dutiful but relished,
brought you peace and comfort.

Even now I see you
testing its sticky fruit,
its sweetness on the tongue.

The Little Drummer Boy Considers a Sabbatical

Don't kid yourself. I know what you're thinking,
"Here he comes again. He and his drum."
I know it's all predictable—the tinsel
Draped like spiders' webs on drooping branches,
The costly cards and breakable displays,
The incandescent camels on the lawns,
And, as if to usher in the lot
Or keep it moving to a steady beat,
The unrelenting rhythm of my drum.
I know you'd like it if I took my drum
And did the thing that's better left unmentioned
Or failing that, packed up my drum and drumsticks
And beat a path to Spain or Yucatan.
Don't think I haven't fathomed your disdain.
"Give it a rest!" I've almost heard you say
And truth to tell, I've more than once considered
Taking a well-earned leave in some warm spot
Where I could drink tequila or champagne
And, if luck should favor me again,
Compose another sentimental song.
But those are dreams, unlikely to come true,
And for the nonce, whatever you may think,
I have a duty and a job to do.
Look at this way, folks: not everyone
Is quite as old or cynical as you,
And though I know that endless repetition
Has put a certain tarnish on my charm,
If there is still a single open soul
With what the Zen-folks call beginner's mind,
Be sure that I'll be there to bring delight
As once I did to you, when you were younger
And heard without dismissal or dislike
The light and gentle tapping of my drum.

33 RPM

Dylan. Cash. Sinatra. Belafonte.
What could have seemed more constant than those voices,
Each a timbre unlike any other?
Not the sentiments their songs expressed
Nor yet their pulsing rhythms held attention
So much as their unprecedented selves,
Embodied in a rasp or lyric tenor,
Rugged bass or spoken baritone.
Who could have known that voices so commanding
Would, in time, grow hoarse or whisper-thin
Or that the selves inhabiting those timbres
Would prove no more enduring than the sough
Of wind, the roll of thunder? Even now
To hear them as they were is to recall
An old solidity of thought and feeling,
As though those cadences preserved in vinyl
Were not mere transitory exhalations
But were as tangible as cooling glass,
The self's original, unchanging vessel.

Leaf, Sunlight, Asphalt

> *"our transient fictions of name and form"*
>   Chris Arthur

Those leaves outside my window
    lift lightly in the wind.
        That newly planted cypress

takes on a deeper greenness.
    This summer heat will pass,
        but here in late July

sunlight warms the foxgloves;
    the asphalt, rinsed by rain,
        looks blacker than before.

How pleasing are those names—
    buddleia, artemisia—
        which in our innocence

we lend to changing things.
    Fictions, yes, and dreams,
        but wholly necessary.

And think how desolate
    this insubstantial world
        would be without its names:

cypress, rain, July
    magnolia, rose, lobelia,
        leaf, sunlight, asphalt.

Western New York, 2008

Merton, were you living at this moment
You wouldn't fail to note how *lucid silence*,
As you once called it, silence void of language
But resonant with unperturbed awareness,
Is growing rarer even as we speak.
In silence, you believed, the hills and forests
Bespoke themselves, absent self or Hearer.
To that condition, which eluded you
Even in your solitary hours,
You made it your vocation to aspire,
Fighting all the while your ego's need
To speak, be recognized, be deemed important.
The hills and forests that you left behind
Are still resounding in their silences
But everywhere, the clamor you decried
Is swelling in a violent crescendo.
Would that you might rejoin us to implore
Our anxious minds to hearken to themselves
And by the eloquence of your example
Enable us to listen and be still.

Irondequoit, Oswego, Canisteo

Piling as they will in mid-October
on unmown grass and still-intact impatiens,

those leaves could be the emblems of the names
that land on hills or settle into valleys

and later take their places on the maps
or in the histories of towns and cities,

as though they were indigenous as oak
or solid as the boulders on a mountain.

Irondequoit. Oswego. Canisteo.
Even to say them is to feel their weight,

though it's composed of little more than air
and though its content, felt or accidental,

may be at best a homely imitation
of things that are themselves no more substantial

than speeches that endured beyond the moment
and once-green forms that crumble underfoot.

A Bow

The here and everywhere, the now and always
of the poetic moment.
    Seamus Heaney

Now without its leaves, that Red-Twig Dogwood
could satisfy an appetite for order,

so unencumbered are its upswept branches,
no two alike but rising from a single

curvature of earth and leaf-strewn snow,
which always was, if not in this one yard

then in that everywhere to which such words
as these are but an homage and a bow.

One Time, One Meeting

Picking up the phone to call my son,
I entertain the thought that every act,
No matter how familiar or banal,
Might be construed as unrepeatable
And all of life as ceremonial.
What could be less formal than the feel
Of yet another handset in the hand
Or, beneath my fingertips, the cool
Resistance to the punching-in of numbers?
And what could be more normal than *hello*,
Spoken by a voice I couldn't fail
To recognize, despite the poor connection,
The fading in and out across the miles?
And yet to entertain that counter-thought,
To see each action and its consequence
As marvelous and not to be repeated,
Suffices to enlarge this conversation
Beyond the casual or circumstantial,
The morning's headlines and the evening's news,
As though just now the truth of things had spoken.

"How Do You Get to Carnegie Hall?"

Who wouldn't fear the darkened concert hall,
The silence settling on expectant faces?
Clammy hands. A turmoil in the belly.
And all because the moment has arrived
When every minute spent on making fingers
Do what they should do, and every hour
Devoted to a notion of perfection
Have brought this cloud-shape sometimes called a self
To just this place, where dreadful things can happen.
Whose music will arise from practised hands?
And who's the one who calmly seats himself,
Adjusts his stand, positions his guitar?
It all depends, his body seems to say,
As though the contours of an allemande
Were not so permanent as they appear
But were the offspring of the changing air,
The progeny of temperature and moisture,
The creatures of the meal he ate this morning.
Better not to dwell on those conditions.
Better to begin, as if this one
Occasion were the only one that mattered,
And what is called a self were but a venue,
An article of faith, a clear volition.

At Notre Dame

Someone has put a hamburger into the hand
Of the stone Jesus conversing with His disciples,
A half-eaten burger still in its paper wrapper,
As if to say that no one must neglect
To eat, even when telling parables
Or comforting His followers, who listen
In attitudes of reverence and ardor.

Expecting Nothing

Even before you were born,
your parents were expecting.
What have you done since then
but meet their expectations
or, as the case may be,
fall short? So now, if I
should ask you for a moment

to live without those framing
goals and stipulations,
those blinding expectations,
my modest proposition
might seem another mandate
which you, for good or ill,
must heed or disregard.

But let me, nonetheless,
invite you to envision
a day without the notions
of parents, priests, and teachers,
a day of rest and leisure
and dauntless exploration—
no lark or summer picnic

but a gate through which, for once,
you might conduct yourself,
seeing, as if you'd never
laid eyes on them before,
the street-sign at the corner
bent at a quirky angle,
the first forsythia

turning from brown to yellow,
the disappearing moon
at seven in the morning.
And should you feel impelled

by temperament or habit
to classify such sights
or assign defining names,

to praise, dispraise, or grade
that stranger's way of walking,
that Chrysler's peeling paint,
that odd, disheveled man,
let me suggest to you
that the clanking garbage truck
expelling noxious fumes,

those potholes left to deepen
for lack of funds or caring,
that elderly volunteer
delivering Meals on Wheels,
those tulips pushing up
through newly loosened soil,
are, at this one moment,

all there is. And as
you cross that dangerous street,
looking from left to right,
let me propose to you
that the venue you will enter,
prepared or unprepared,
in your envisioned future

will be no foreign field
nor alien terrain
but a self to which you've come
exactly as you are.
In time that formless form,
composed of mind and limb,
desire and circumstance,

may prosper and acquire
stature, rank, and power.
But may you also step
lightly into the light
of yet another morning
and into the stranger light
of dusk, expecting nothing.

For the Phi Beta Kappa Initiation Ceremony
Alfred University, April 7, 2004

Right Livelihood
On the occasion of my retirement

How shall I address you,
you to whom I gave
my youth, my middle age,
and much of my regard?
Now that I'm taking leave

of you, and you are backing
swiftly away from me,
how shall I name your features,
which even now recede,
as does the din of voices,

the clamor of demands?
What shall I call you now,
you who were not opaque
nor ever very solid,
your meetings, consultations,

syllabi, appointments
at most an aggregate
to which the name Professor
attached itself, as if
to give that ever-shifting

scaffolding of duties
and transitory desires
a look of permanence
and lasting aspiration?
Say, if you will, that all

those hours disappearing
even as I write,
those hours spent preparing
to say what might be said
of metaphor or meter,

O'Faolain's ironies
or Yeats's layered symbols,
do not reside in fraying
folders, yellowed notes
or boxes in a closet,

but are as living beings
inhabiting the wakened
minds of Claire and Jason,
Scott and Domenica,
and all those other seekers

who trusted me to listen
and, when apt, to guide
their nascent understandings
into a lit arena
or call to their attention

channels that otherwise
might never have been opened.
To them I dedicate
these lines, as well I might,
for in their widened hearts

and slow-maturing minds
is my continuation.
But what shall I say to *you*,
my erstwhile Superintendent,
who summoned me to quarrels

I'd rather have avoided
and when it suited you
subjected me to judgments
better left unspoken?
On more than one occasion

Larkin called you Toad,
a graceless epithet,
though not entirely false.
Frog, I might have said,
though not the frog that brought

enlightenment to Basho.
Rather, the one who croaks
in low, unmannerly tones
whenever he is hungry
or longing for his way.

I might have other names,
not all of them benign,
but today the crocuses
are up, and casting glances
backward or askance

is not my inclination.
So let me take a leaf
from Basho's heritage
and call you by a name
reserved for such employment

as does more good than harm,
a name appropriate
to rescuers and monks,
priests and clowns alike.
Right Livelihood, it's called,

and though your character
is not a priest's or hero's
much less a martyred saint's,
the livelihood you offered
was right enough for me,

providing as it did
a forum for reminding
the most recalcitrant
that every waking moment
is worthy of attention

and worthy, too, of words
chosen with precision
and truthful to the core.
Right speech, it's sometimes called,
by which is meant the speech

that indicates what's there
and never what is not;
that waters seeds of joy
and equanimity;
and, when warranted,

assigns revealing names
to greed and cruelty,
injustice and deceit.
So let me raise a cup
in gratitude to you,

Right Livelihood, who fostered
right and noble speech
in all of us who sought it,
as though it were your offspring,
your one enduring son.

April, 2006

Not Yet

Give me, if you will, a little time
To understand how meanings come and go,
Resembling ants converging at an anthill
And then dispersing, each with work to do.
Meanwhile, the anthill rises and expands.
The sun comes out. The days grow ever shorter.

Give me time to sense how meanings perish
Like plums left unattended in a bowl.
Because their lives were finite in the first place,
That spreading mold should come as no surprise.
So it is with meanings, I suppose,
Though how and why I've yet to understand.

Uncollected Poems

Ubi Caritas

The corn was orient and immortal wheat . . .
The dust and stones of the street were as precious as gold.
    TRAHERNE, *Centuries of Meditations*

  i

How easily it ended:
how readily that light
went out, taking its early
radiance into a place
I couldn't enter. Then,
the secular barrenness—
the river without a heart
or artery, the waters
suitable for plunder.
And in the home, the rift
no one would speak about:
the broken stem, the shaft
of unqualified belief
fractured, as if a quake
had faulted it where it stood.

  ii

I remember the river's smells—
oil and gasoline,
the rotting carp, the trash
on the sand the morning after.
What could inhabit cans,
fish-skeletons, and shells
in the absence of belief?
In place of immanence
there came a backwash, fraught
with history's debris.
Here was no orient wheat
nor dreaded godhead risen

out of a river's darkness,
but the bleak ephemeral waste
of a failing river town.

iii

Crinklings of India paper
under a moistened thumb.
And the damp loam of names—
Ruth, Gethsemane—
familiar and strange.
Those ardors of the Word
that informed a limestone path
or a leaf with the spirit's light
and infused the touch of hands
with a love beyond our knowing,
dispersed themselves in doubts,
analyses, regrets—
as though a stone had dried
or a drink had lost its savor.

iv

Imperious, replete
with self-congratulation,
my brazen intellect
alloyed a precious metal.
At the river's edge I saw
no golden paving stones
but an iridescent coin
on contaminated water.
Yet, in the sanctity
of dreams and in the shut
chambers of meditation,
the openings remained—
pinholes casting light
in a *camera obscura*,
white rings on murky water.

v

And here at a meeting point
of ardor and regret,
I think of the river's weight
breaking against the dam,
of shells and refuse strewn
where water cleansed the spillway.
How could I not have known
that belief is not a shaft
but a spring become a stream
become a river, bearing
the intellect's detritus
into a place where water
widens, and light elects
the pure and impure alike.

The High Studio at Yaddo

Too many feet have climbed these wooden steps,
Worn to a lighter color in the middle,
And too many writers, sure or not so sure
Of what they might elect to put on paper,
Once they have made this spacious room their home,
Have spent an hour or an afternoon
Looking at the fountain or the lawn
Or at the light persisting through the pines
Or, if the day is clear, the distant mountain.

What is a stanza but an empty room,
Waiting no less patiently than this one
To be inhabited by someone new,
Who knows too well the history of those
Who've come before, but nonetheless assumes
The robes of temporal authority,
Filling the closet with his rumpled clothes
And spreading out his books, his stacks of notes,
As though he held the title to his room
And all he would discover were his own.

Intrusion
for Robin

Though it was nothing but a heavy wind
rattling the sashes of my bedroom window
and scattering debris, it brought to mind
a snowy mountain in New Mexico,
the two of us suspended on a cable
above the rocks, our shadow growing smaller,
and both of us imagining the fall.
Held up by nothing but a wooden floor,
we swung between two towers, holding on.
How readily that momentary fear
called up its memory in lung and bone,
occasioned by a wind against a dormer.
No larger than a surgical incision,
it made its point, its violent intrusion.

Morning in Beara

1

Friend of my heart, I write to you this morning
From this remote retreat beside the ocean,
Thinking it better that we correspond,
However haltingly, than that we wait
In separate quarters for some grand reunion.
This rocky landscape, rich in purple heather
But poor in soil, sparse in population,
Could tell the story of a soul's defeat
Or more historically, a parable
Of stony poverty and mute survival.
Yet in the ample light of late July
The blood-red petals of the wild fuchsia,
Cascading by the thousands down the cliffside,
Insist against the evidence of hardship
That even in the stoniest environs
The life-force will be heard from and the truth
Will out. This morning, over Bantry Bay,
The first pink streaks are breaking through the cloudbank
And casting on the pewter-colored water
A radiance that some would call the spirit's
And others would appreciate as light
On light, as color modulating color.
Soon enough, the fishing-boats will come,
Their lights still on, their dark shapes beating forward,
And looking from this vantage point like insects
Proceeding slowly down a foggy pane—
Or like the steady movement of a pen
Across the page, its will no less insistent,
Its course no less dependent on desire.

II

    Some days the silence here is nearly total
And the first bird, arriving at my window
And chirping once or twice, can seem uncommon,
A small event made large by circumstance,
A drink of water spreading through the cells,
A sudden and auspicious irrigation.
But to recall that sudden transformation
Is also to recall a Friday morning
Some twenty years ago, when I went walking
Into the little town I've spoken of—
The quiet seaside town where once a year
I spent a fortnight reading spacious novels
And basking in the heat of early August,
Watching waves or following the progress
Of words across a page. I couldn't say
What prompted me that morning to abandon
My wooden chair, unless it was the glare
Of sunlight on the water or the cries
Of children chasing dogs and kicking sand.
Whatever it may have been, it drove me off
The sun-drenched beach and into the shady town
Where men in shorts and women wearing sunhats
Greeted me with looks of recognition
If not quite warmth, their eyes acknowledging
My presence but their bodies gliding forward,
An attitude consistent with my status
As visitor but leaving me in silence
And making of my walk a moving depot
Through which the trains were passing, one by one.
Perhaps it was my solitude, accepted
If not quite chosen, which directed me
Across the street and past the hardware store,
The butcher's shop, the corner grocery,
And up stone steps, to where a postal clerk
Dispensed stamps and chatted with a man
Who had, it seemed, no business to attend to,
No dog to walk or engine to repair.

And as I waited, my impatience showing,
My footsole tapping on the hardwood floor,
It dawned on me that someone stood behind me,
A little to my left, half-visible
And, I sensed, half-recognizable
If only to a heightened intuition.
I turned enough to catch a glimpse of shoulders,
A sunken chin, a gray receding hairline,
A wrinkled hat cocked back above a forehead,
And eyes which seemed to temper what they saw.
Our glances met. We awkwardly exchanged
The phrases one coughs up on such occasions,
Trite as they are but better than those pauses
Born of shyness or ineptitude.
And here the words we uttered signified
More than a cordial greeting. Before me stood
A man with whom I'd laughed, confided stories,
And broken bread until our falling out—
And subsequent to that, the perfect silence
Which we, as former friends, had built of stone
And dourly maintained for half a decade,
A monument to spite and injured pride.
"Edward," I said, as if to say his name
Would be sufficient to unlock those voices
Which even in the aftermath of friendship
Somehow stay alive, their quiet pleadings
Heard in the solitude of meditation
And echoed in the texts of unsent letters
Or couched in speeches, endlessly rehearsed
And spoken to an audience of one.
No thunder rolled, nor did the hardwood floor
Open beneath our feet. But in his eyes
I thought I saw a flash of recognition,
A ray of light, which had it been a voice
Would not have kept its silence any longer
But spoken of regret and wasted love,
The tamping down of memory and fondness,
The stirrings of residual affection.

As it happened, neither of us spoke
Of anything so intimate as that
But talked, as men will do, of politics
And government, congressional elections,
The local mayor's fatuous remarks
On public education. And when the line
Moved forward and our conversation ended,
I wondered at how much had gone unsaid,
How many dormant roots had been awakened
But left to flower at a later time.
And though our tentative, constricted handshake
Partook of stiffness and finality,
It seemed that something frozen had been loosened
Or that another country had been heard from,
A country which has yet to seal its borders
Or study war, so fertile are its fields
And so remote its unpolluted waters.

III

   Seldom eloquent and often silent,
My father spoke with equanimity,
Or so it seemed, his temperate demeanor
Interpreted by some as lack of passion
But no less often as the fruit of wisdom,
A little overripe perhaps, but welcome
Amidst the noise and frenzy of the school
Where he was principal and sometimes parent
To children learning to be sociable,
Their raucous laughs erupting from the playground,
Their woes and battles, grievances and gripes
Arriving without warning at his door.
Likewise his silence seemed to his detractors
A vacant room, a hollow disappointment
But now, in retrospect, it most resembles
The quiet burning of a pilot light,
Unnoticed, inconspicuous, abiding,
But no less integral or capable
Of bringing dormant energies to life.

How else explain the subtle transformation
I witnessed as I sat beside his bed,
The nurses elsewhere and the relatives
Departed, leaving the two of us to settle
Whatever quarrels, spoken or unspoken,
Had come between a father and his son.
The room was small and smelled of disinfectants.
A little light—the light of late November—
Was streaming through the curtain. Had he not
Deprived me, as a child, of those material
Comforts which a schoolman couldn't afford?
The question came from somewhere known to him
But not to me, so little had I felt
Deprived of anything. But had I not
Imposed on him my nascent social conscience
And in my brash self-righteous adolescence
Accused him of a dozen grave transgressions
For which, if anyone, a generation
Should take the blame and not the private man?
Perhaps I had, he said, but if I had
It didn't matter. Such were the words exchanged
Between us, all our barriers removed,
Our differences no thicker than the glass
Of water catching light beside his bed.
But what I want, if possible, to describe
Is how in that last portion of his life,
His strength and spirit savagely diminished,
He found within his stricken constitution
A gift of speech, a sudden eloquence
Which I would liken to a mountain stream
Or more precisely, to a river's source
Somewhere in the north. "I always thought
That you'd become a shining light. But you
Were always rather reticent on that point."
Whatever voice it was that spoke those words
It came from some remote, uncharted region
Which may not be so different from this stark
Peninsula, whose mountainous horizon

Is in its fashion reticent but shining
And holds within its wild, unyielding rock
The spirit of a father come to light.

   IV

   It sometimes happens after many years
Away from some archaic habitat
That I encounter it again, not only
In dreams and indolent imaginings
But also in the flesh—or should I say
The wood and pitted stone. Such was the case
One summer morning when I took myself
Back to a fieldstone church in County Clare
And there encountered in its sunlit churchyard,
Where simple graves kept company with pompous
Monuments and listing Celtic crosses,
An image of a man whom I remember
Picking his way through moss and uncut grass,
Observed by grazing sheep and who knows which
Unfriendly deity. That man, of course,
Was I—or else a version of the I
Who wakes from fitful dreams to sip his coffee
And write his letters to those absent friends
Who are in truth but versions of the selves
Whom he, in all good faith, can now remember
Only as shades and disembodied voices.
But there he walked, that version of myself,
And there I walked as well, the northern light
Yellowing the letters on the headstones
And brightening the path beneath my feet.
I tell you this, in part, to celebrate
A curious reunion. There we walked,
The two of us, as though the past and present
Were partners in some enigmatic errand
And not two islands in a northern sea,
Signaling at night but otherwise
Apart. I tell you this, as well, because

It all came back to me this foggy morning
As I was looking out across the water
And waiting for the beacon in the lighthouse
At Mizen Head to weaken and dissolve
Into the morning light. And while I thought
Of that congruency in County Clare
And saw those two, in tandem, walking there,
I found myself remembering the morning
In mid-November when my son was born,
A chilly day but not without its moments
Of brilliant light on gray decaying leaves.
I saw the waiting room, the magazines,
And heard the swishing of the double doors
As nurses came and went, the heels on tile,
The doctors' low, inaudible exchanges.
I waited seven hours. Then came the news,
The calling of the newly christened father
Into a garish room. There lay an infant
Wrapped in blankets, nestled by his mother,
And looking half-bewildered by the world.
How shall I describe to you the strange
Amalgam of uneasiness and joy
That rose in me when I drew close to them
And making bold to cradle in my arms
The wrinkled one whom I would call my son,
Saw in his face the features of my father?
It seemed that something gone had come again—
Or, to put it otherwise, that features
To which I once attached the name of father
Had gone into seclusion for a time
And now returned, refreshed by hibernation
And sharpened by the early-morning light.

V

   To spend an hour looking out on water,
Aware of waves forming and re-forming
And seeing in their openings and closings
An image of creation and extinction,

Is to be tutored, wave by dissolving wave,
And succored by the movement of those white,
Expanding lines, which catch the morning wind
And widen like a steady exhalation.
Strange to be sustained by breaking waves,
Which in their rise resemble human passion
And in their fall resemble those departures
For which no elegy is adequate
Nor letter home sufficient to console.
Stranger still to think of you this morning,
Not as the friend who packed his worldly goods
And bid farewell to all, including me,
But as the friend who met me at the station,
A little worn, perhaps, but no less ready
To take up our enduring conversation,
Which suffers absences and silences
And has its own white foam, its own momentum.
Where are the words to honor that resurgence
Of energy in friendship long neglected?
Better, I think, to let my voice fall silent
Before the spectacle of crashing water—
Or if I must, to write you from this outpost
And tell you what I saw as I was dumping
Ashes from my stove and finding sticks
To light another fire. Scraping out
The last gray chunks and fashioning a bed
Of splintered wood, a pyramid of turf,
I watched the nascent flame take hold and spread
Upward through the shelter I'd created,
Which soon enough collapsed, consumed by flame
And lending to the early-morning hour
A complement of warmth, a sweet aroma.
Call it if you will the flame of passion,
Which throws out heat but leaves the world in ashes.
Or call it, more constructively, the flame
Of amity, so easily extinguished
And yet so capable of shedding light
And softening, if only for a time,
The harsher edges of a frigid room.

Acknowledgments

Acknowledgements are due to the following publications in which some of these poems were previously published:

Agenda, Amicus Journal, Carolina Quarterly, Chelsea, Cithara, Cortland Review, Dharma Connection, Georgia Review, Iowa Review, Kenyon Review, Midwest Quarterly, Mississippi Valley Review, New England Review, New Hibernia Review, North American Review, OnEarth, Ontario Review, Poetica, Poetry, Poetry Ireland Review, Poetry Miscellany, Prairie Schooner, The Formalist, The Recorder, Seneca Review, Sewanee Review, Shenandoah, Southern Humanities Review, Terrain, TriQuarterly, Unsplendid.

"NotYet" was printed as a broadside by Jerry Reddan at the Tangram Press (Berkeley, California).

"Ubi Caritas" was printed in the chapbook *The Other Shore* (1991) by Wesley Tanner at Passim Editions (Ann Arbor, Michigan).

Photo of Ben Howard by Robin Caster Howard

BEN HOWARD is Emeritus Professor of English at Alfred University. For the past four decades, he has contributed poems, reviews, essays, and articles to leading journals in Ireland, England, and America. His numerous awards include the Milton Dorfman Award in Poetry, the Theodore Christian Hoepfner Award, and a fellowship from the National Endowment for the Arts. He is the author of nine previous books, most recently *The Backward Step: Essays on Zen Practice* (Whitlock, 2014). Visit his website at www.howardbw.com and his blog at www.practiceofzen.com.